The ESSEN

BUSINESS
STATISTICS II

Louise J. Clark, Ph.D.

Professor of Business Statistics
Jacksonville State University, Jacksonville, Alabama

This book is a continuation of *"THE ESSENTIALS OF BUSINESS STATISTICS I"* and begins with Chapter 8. It covers the usual course outline of Business Statistics II. Earlier/basic topics are covered in *"THE ESSENTIALS OF BUSINESS STATISTICS I"*.

Research and Education Association
61 Ethel Road West
Piscataway, New Jersey 08854

THE ESSENTIALS® OF BUSINESS STATISTICS II

Printed in the United States of America

Library of Congress Catalog Card Number 90-61822

International Standard Book Number 0–87891–842-6

WHAT "THE ESSENTIALS" WILL DO FOR YOU

This book is a review and study guide. It is comprehensive and it is concise.

It helps in preparing for exams, in doing homework, and remains a handy reference source at all times.

It condenses the vast amount of detail characteristic of the subject matter and summarizes the **essentials** of the field.

It will thus save hours of study and preparation time.

The book provides quick access to the important principles, theorems, concepts, and equations in the field.

Materials needed for exams can be reviewed in summary form – eliminating the need to read and re-read many pages of textbook and class notes. The summaries will even tend to bring detail to mind that had been previously read or noted.

This "ESSENTIALS" book has been prepared by an expert in the field, and has been carefully reviewed to assure accuracy and maximum usefulness.

Dr. Max Fogiel
Program Director

CONTENTS

CHAPTER 8

ADDITIONAL TOPICS IN HYPOTHESIS TESTING

8.1 TESTING TWO POPULATION MEANS

Testing to determine if two population means are identical with respect to a certain characteristic involves a process similar to that used when testing whether one population mean is equal to some prespecified value. That is, we may develop a procedure for performing a two population mean test with the same steps we used when testing only one population parameter. The only difference in applying this procedure is that the equations used to calculate either a t-value or a Z-value will be different from those used in the case of only one population. As a review, we will use five steps in our hypothesis testing procedure, as outlined below.

Step 1. State the null hypothesis and the alternative hypothesis. The null hypothesis is the statement which we test, while the alternative hypothesis is the statement which past history or the literature might support, or possibly, simply the belief of the individual performing the test. The null hypothesis and the alternative hypothesis must reflect opposite beliefs or assumptions. Remember that the null hypothesis is the *assumption* which we set up to test. Examples of possible hypotheses setups for two population mean tests are:

    1. $H_0: \mu_1 = \mu_2$

          $H_1: \mu_1 \neq \mu_2$ (2-tailed test)

          This setup is used when we are testing only for a significant difference between the two population means and the direction is not important.

2. $H_0: \mu_1 \geq \mu_2$

$H_1: \mu_1 < \mu_2$ (1-tailed test)

This setup is used when we are interested in determining if the mean of population 1 is truly less than the mean of population 2.

3. $H_0: \mu_1 \leq \mu_2$

$H_1: \mu_1 > \mu_2$ (1-tailed test)

This setup is used when we are interested in determining if the mean of population 1 is truly greater than the mean of population 2.

Step 2. Specify the values stated in the problem.

Step 3. Determine the appropriate distribution (either the standard normal Z-distribution, or Student's t-distribution) and an appropriate tabled value.

Step 4. Solve for the value of Z or t (whichever is appropriate) using the appropriate equation for the values involved.

Step 5. Draw a conclusion as to whether H_0 should be rejected, or not.

Rule: For a 2-tailed test, if the absolute value of the computed value from Step 4 is greater than or equal to the table from Step 3, reject the null hypothesis (H_0:) and accept the alternative hypothesis (H_1:). Otherwise, fail to reject the null hypothesis (H_0:), which requires no action to be taken regarding H_1:. This is simply an indication that the sample results are not sufficient to allow us to reject the null hypothesis; really, almost a lack of a conclusion. For a 1-tailed test, the proper modification needs to be made (i.e., no absolute value).

When tests involve two population means, the assumption is that random samples are selected from each population and that the mean calculated from each of the two samples estimates the respective population mean. The difference in sample means is, therefore, used in the calculation of either Z or t, and the sampling distribution of this statistic is referred to as the *sampling distribution of differences in sample means* ($\bar{x}_1 - \bar{x}_2$). As was discussed in Chapter 5 of *The Essentials of Business Statistics I* for the sample case, according to the central limit theorem, the distribution of all possible sample means for a given situation approaches a normal distribution if the sample size is at least 30. The same holds true for the sample distribution of $\bar{x}_1 - \bar{x}_2$; i.e., if the two random samples consist of at least 30 units each (and if they are independent this means that the sampling units from one population are selected independently from those of the second population), then the distribution of all possible differences between sample means will also approach a normal distribution. Therefore, these conditions allow for the use of the following Z-statistic when the standard deviations of both populations (σ_1 and σ_2) are known.

$$Z = \frac{\bar{x}_1 - \bar{x}_2}{\sigma_{\bar{x}_1 - \bar{x}_2}}$$

where: $\sigma_{\bar{x}_1 - \bar{x}_2} = \sqrt{\sigma_1^2/n_1 + \sigma_1^2/n_2}$

and is called the standard error of the difference between sample means.

When the population standard deviations (σ_1 and σ_2) are not known, which is generally the case, the values of the sample standard deviations (S_1 and S_2) are used as replacements. When this is the case, the value of t is calculated as follows:

$$t = \frac{\bar{x}_1 - \bar{x}_2}{\hat{\sigma}_{\bar{x}_1 - \bar{x}_2}},$$

where: $\sigma_{\bar{x}_1 - \bar{x}_2} = \sqrt{\sigma_1^2 / n_1 + S_2^2 / n}$

EXAMPLE:

The Dressit Corporation developed an advertising campaign which was directed toward the male population. After the initiation of the campaign, the Dressit advertising manager wished to determine if the campaign had truly appealed more to males than females. Thus, he decided to compare the average purchase amounts of the advertised products by male vs. female buyers. Gender information was collected at the time of the sale. He randomly selected 100 males and determined that the average amount they spent since the advertising campaign began was $987. He also randomly selected 100 females and found that the average purchase amount of this group was $1050. Since there was no knowledge of population standard deviations, he also computed the sample standard deviation for each group. The standard deviation for the 100 males was $25 and the standard deviation for the females was $10. Can the advertising manager conclude that there is a difference in the campaign's effectiveness for males and females based on purchase amount? Test at the .05 level of significance.

1. State the null and alternative hypotheses.

$H_0: \mu_1 = \mu_2$

$H_1: \mu_1 \neq \mu_2$ (2-tailed test)

We use this setup because the problem asked us to determine only if the average purchase differed and did not specify that we are interested in a directional difference.

2. Specify the values stated in the problem.

$n_1 = 100$ $\qquad\qquad$ $n_2 = 100$

$\bar{x}_1 = \$987$ $\qquad\qquad$ $\bar{x}_2 = \$1050$

$S_1 = \$25$ $\qquad\qquad$ $S_2 = \$10$

$\alpha = .05$

(level of significance)

3. Determine the appropriate distribution and a value from the appropriate table.

In this case, the t-distribution is appropriate. This is due to the fact that we are estimating the standard deviations. The degrees of freedom for t should be $(100 - 1) + (100 - 1) = 198$. In practice, a t with 198 degrees of freedom is quite close to the Z-distribution, so we may use Z. Here we are using a two-tailed test because the alternative hypothesis is $\neq$; therefore, we must place half of the value of α (.05) in each tail of the curve so that we may determine the area from the tail to the mean and subsequently determine the appropriate value of Z from the table.

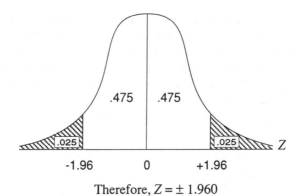

.475   .475

.025   .025 Z

-1.96   0   +1.96

Therefore, $Z = \pm 1.960$

4. Solve for the value of Z.

$$Z = \frac{\bar{x}_1 - \bar{x}_2}{\hat{\sigma}_{\bar{x}_1 - \bar{x}_2}} \quad ,$$

where: $\hat{\sigma}_{\bar{x}_1 - \bar{x}_2} = \sqrt{S_1^2/n_1 = S_2^2/n_2}$.

$$Z = \frac{987 - 1050}{\sqrt{(25)^2/100 = (10)^2/100}}$$

$$= \frac{-63}{2.6926}$$

$$= -23.4.$$

5. Draw a conclusion.

Since $| {-23.4} |$ is greater than $| \pm 1.96 |$, we should reject the null hypothesis (H_0:) and accept the alternative hypothesis (H_1:). This allows the advertising manager to conclude that there is a difference between the average amount purchased by males and females. It does not, however, allow him to conclude a directional difference; i.e., he cannot state that the advertising campaign was significantly more effective for either group. As a matter of fact, these sample results should not lead him to conclude that his campaign definitely hit the target. The females' average purchase was greater than that of the males, but he can't conclude that it is significantly greater since he did not design his test in this fashion. He could retest, however, using a directional hypothesis. Note also that there is a chance that the wrong conclusion has been reached. The level of significance (α) is the probability of rejecting a true null hypothesis. Therefore, even though we have concluded that a difference exists, there is a 5% chance that we have concluded this in error. Another way of expressing this concept is that there is a 5% chance that we have made a Type I error.

We may also come to the same conclusion by using a graphic or pictorial approach. That is, we can label our Z-curve appropriately relative to rejection regions and fail-to-reject region, and place the computed value from Step 4 appropriately along the Z-axis as illustrated below (not drawn to scale).

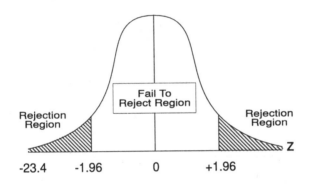

Note that -23.4 falls well out into the rejection region, again calling for a rejection of the null hypothesis (H_0:).

8.2   TESTING TWO POPULATION PROPORTIONS

Hypothesis tests involving two population proportions are performed very much like those involving two population means. The same five step process may be used; however, notational differences must be taken into account. When stating the null and alternative hypotheses in Step 1, they will be stated as follows.

1. H_0: $\pi_1 = \pi_2$

   H_1: $\pi_1 \neq \pi_2$ (2-tailed test)

   This setup is used when testing for a significant difference between the proportion of some characteristic in two populations. No directional difference is implied.

2. H_0: $\pi_1 \geq \pi_2$

   H_1: $\pi_1 < \pi_2$ (1-tailed test)

   This setup is used if we are interested in determining if the proportion of some characteristic in population 1 is less than the proportion of that same characteristic in population 2.

3. H_0: $\pi_1 \leq \pi_2$

   H_1: $\pi_1 > \pi_2$ (1-tailed test)

   This setup is used if we are interested in determining if the proportion of some characteristic in population 1 is greater than the proportion of that same characteristic in population 2.

Also, the equation for calculating the Z-statistic in Step 4 will have to conform to proportion notation.

$$Z = \frac{P_1 - P_2}{\hat{S}_{p_1 - p_2}},$$

where: $\hat{\sigma}_{p_1 - p_2} = \sqrt{\hat{\pi}(1 - \hat{\pi})\left(\frac{1}{n_1} + \frac{1}{n_2}\right)}$

(standard error of the distribution) and

$$\hat{\pi} = \frac{n_1 p_1 + n_2 p_2}{n_1 + n_2}.$$

The Z-test is appropriate when n_1 and n_2 are both 30 or larger due to the central limit theorem. Recall that the conditions: $n_1 p_1 \geq 5$, $n_1(1 - p_1) \geq$

$5, n_2 p_2 \geq 5$, and $n_2(1-p_2) \geq 5$ are also required for the normality assumption when dealing with proportions. When these conditions hold, the sampling distribution of the differences in proportions $(P_1 - P_2)$ is approximately normally distributed.

EXAMPLE:

The President of First City Bank would like to know if the proportion of customers who have CDs with his bank is at least as great as the proportion of Savings and Loan Company customers who have CDs with that organization. A study is conducted in which a random sample of 500 First City Bank customers is compared with a random sample of 350 Savings and Loan Company customers. The results from the samples indicate that 150 of the bank's customers had CDs with the bank while 140 of the loan company's customers had CDs with that organization. Test to determine if the proportion having CDs with the bank is significantly less than the proportion having CDs with the loan company. Perform this test at the .01 level of significance.

1. State the null and alternative hypotheses.

$H_0 : \pi_1 \geq \pi_2$

$H_1 : \pi_1 < \pi_2$ (1-tailed test)

This setup is used due to the fact that we want to know if the proportion in population 1 is truly less than the proportion in population 2. However, we assume initially in the null hypothesis that this is not the case.

2. Specify the values given in the problem.

$n_1 = 500$ $\qquad\qquad$ $n_2 = 350$

$x_1 = 150$ $\qquad\qquad$ $x_2 = 140$

$\alpha = .01$

Using these values, we determine that:

$p_1 = x_1/n_1$ $\qquad\qquad$ $p_2 = x_2/n_2$

$\quad = 150/500$ $\qquad\qquad \quad = 140/350$

$\quad = .30$ $\qquad\qquad\qquad\quad = .40.$

3. Determine the appropriate distribution and a value from the appropriate table.

Here, the Z-distribution is used due to the central limit theorem.

$$n_1 = 500 \qquad\qquad\qquad n_2 = 350$$

$$n_1 p_1 = 500\,(.30) = 150 \geq 5 \qquad n_2 p_2 = 350\,(.40) = 140 \geq 5$$

$$n_1(1-p_1) = 500\,(.7) = 350 \geq 5 \qquad n_2(1-p_2) = 350\,(.60) = 210 \geq 5$$

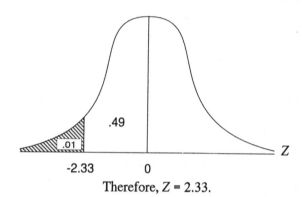

Therefore, $Z = 2.33$.

Note here that the value of α (.01) is placed in the left tail of the curve. This is due to the fact that we are using a one-tailed test and the alternative hypothesis (H_1:) has the less-than sign. When the alternative hypothesis carries the greater-than sign, the α value is placed in the right tail.

    4.   Calculate the value of Z.

$$Z = \frac{P_1 - P_2}{\hat{\sigma}_{P_1 - P_2}},$$

where: $\quad \hat{\sigma}_{P_1 - P_2} = \sqrt{\hat{\pi}(1-\hat{\pi})\left(\dfrac{1}{n_1} + \dfrac{1}{n_2}\right)}$

and $\quad \hat{\pi} = \dfrac{n_1 p_1 + n_2 p_2}{n_1 + n_2}.$

Therefore, working in reverse order:

$$\hat{\pi} = \frac{500(.30) + 350(.40)}{500 + 350} = .341,$$

$$\hat{\sigma}_{p_1 - p_2} = \sqrt{(.341)(1 - .341)(1/500 + 1/350)} = .033,$$

$$Z = \frac{.30 - .40}{.033}$$

$$= -3.03.$$

5. Draw a conclusion.

Since –3.03 < 2.33, we should reject the null hypothesis $(H_0:)$ and accept the alternative hypothesis $(H_1:)$. The alternative hypothesis says that $\pi_1 < \pi_2$; therefore, we conclude that it is true that the proportion of bank customers with CDs is less than the proportion of savings and loan customers. However, there is a .01 chance that this conclusion is in error.

As with the example illustrating two population means, we can show our conclusion graphically or pictorially. It should be observed that since the tail of the curve containing α always makes up the rejection region, that, here again, the value of -3.03 will fall along the Z-axis in the rejection region; -3.03 falls farther away from the mean than does the table value of -2.33.

8.3 SMALL SAMPLE TESTS - TWO POPULATION MEANS

In Chapter 7 of *Essentials of Business Statistics I*, we discussed and illustrated how the Student's *t*-distribution is used to test a population mean when the sample size is not sufficient to invoke the central limit theorem. The two population test for means follows the same reasoning and requires the same conditions as that specified in the case where one population mean is being tested against a prespecified constant. When the two populations being tested are normally distributed, with unknown standard deviations, and when sample sizes of less than 30 are selected, the *t*-distribution may be used to test either for a significant difference or for a directional difference between the two population means. This test is valid, however, only if the two population standard deviations are equal ($\sigma_1 = \sigma_2$). When all these conditions hold, the test statistic conforms to the Student's t-distribution.

$$t = \frac{\bar{x}_1 - \bar{x}_2}{S_{\bar{x}_1 - \bar{x}_2}} \qquad\qquad t = \frac{\bar{x}_1 - \bar{x}_2}{S_{\bar{x}_1 - \bar{x}_2}}$$

where: $S_{\bar{x}_1 - \bar{x}_2} = \sqrt{\dfrac{n_1 s_1^2 + n_2 s_2^2}{n_1 + n_2 - 2}\left(\dfrac{1}{n_1} + \dfrac{1}{n_2}\right)}$, where: $S_{\bar{x}_1 - \bar{x}_2} = \sqrt{\dfrac{n_1 s_1^2 + n_2 s_2^2}{n_1 + n_2 - 2}\left(\dfrac{1}{n_1} + \dfrac{1}{n_2}\right)}$,

which is the standard error of the difference between sample means. The number of degrees of freedom is specified by:

$$df = n_1 + n_2 - 2.$$

The same five step outline as used in the two previous situations will also be used in this case. The following example illustrates a problem of this type.

EXAMPLE:

Food Club Association operates a number of grocery stores. The sales manager claims that Store A's customers, on the average, buy a greater amount of groceries than do those who shop with Store B, located in a similar setting. In order to determine if he is correct, the sales manager randomly selects a number of sales tickets from each store and finds the following. From the 25 tickets selected from Store A, the average (mean) amount per ticket was $54, with a standard deviation of $5. The 20 customers sampled from Store B revealed an average (mean) value to be $51 with a standard deviation of $3. Test at the .01 level of significance to determine if the sales manager's claim is valid. Assume that sales for each store follow a normal distribution.

Step 1. State the null and alternative hypotheses.

$$H_0: \mu_1 \leq \mu_2$$

$$H_1: \mu_1 > \mu_2 \text{ (1-tailed test)}$$

This setup is used because we want to know if the average value in population 1 is truly greater than that in population 2. Initially, however, we assume that this is not the case.

Step 2. Specify values given in the problem.

$$n_1 = 25 \qquad\qquad n_2 = 20$$

$$x_1 = \$54 \qquad\qquad x_2 = \$51$$
$$S_1 = \$5 \qquad\qquad S_2 = \$3$$
$$\alpha = .01$$

Step 3. Determine the appropriate distribution and value from the appropriate table.

In this problem the Student's t-distribution is appropriate. This is due to:

    a. Normally distributed populations, as specified in the problem.

    b. Unknown population standard deviations; the sample standard deviations are used as estimates of these unknown population values.

    c. Each sample size is less than 30.

    d. Although we have not verified this, another assumption of the t-distribution when testing two populations is that the population variances (σ_1^2, σ_2^2) are identical.

$$\begin{aligned} df &= n_1 + n_2 - 2 \\ &= 25 + 20 - 2 \\ &= 43 \end{aligned}$$

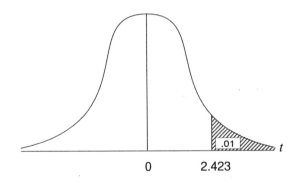

Therefore, $t = 2.423$, as determined from
the student's t-distribution table,
using $\alpha = .01$ and 43 degrees of freedom.

Step 4. Solve for the value of t.

$$t = \frac{\bar{x}_1 - \bar{x}_2}{\sqrt{\left[\left(n_1 s_1^2 + n_2 s_1^2\right)/\left(n_1 + n_2\right)\right]\left(1/n_1 + 1/n_2\right)}}$$

$$t = \frac{54 - 51}{\sqrt{\left[\left(25(5)^2 + 20(3)^2\right)/(20 + 25)\right]\left(1/25 + 1/20\right)}}$$

$$= \frac{3}{\sqrt{\left[(625 + 180)/45\right]/(.04 + .05)}}$$

$$= \frac{3}{\sqrt{17.889(.09)}}$$

$$= 3/1.269$$

$$= 2.364$$

Step 5. Draw a conclusion.

Since 2.364 < 2.423, we cannot reject H_0:, which indicates that the sales manager's claim is not substantiated at this time. That is, the results from these samples are inconclusive, i.e., they are not sufficient to support his claim that customers who shop Store A spend more than those who shop Store B. If he wants to continue to investigate this situation, he should gather additional data and perform the test again.

As we have seen with earlier examples, this same conclusion would be reached if we placed the computed value of 2.364 appropriately along the t-axis. In this case, it would fall in the "fail to reject" region, since the rejection region is always in the tail of the curve.

8.4 PAIRED - SAMPLE TEST

In the previous section, we discussed the situation of testing two population means when the samples were independent of each other. Independence means that the selection of units from one sample has no effect on the selection of units from the other sample. In this section, we are dealing with the opposite case; i.e., here, the sampling units are going to be matched or paired based on some characteristic of interest. Examples of situations which might fit this type of problem are: (1) a pre-test, post-test analysis in which an individual is measured prior to the performance of an experiment and then again after the experiment has been conducted; (2) a test involving sets of twins in which each twin is treated with a different method; (3) husband-wife teams used as matched or paired samples.

The analysis in the paired sample case may be thought of as a spin-off from the one sample t-test, since the statistic of interest is the difference between the matched pairs as opposed to the individual values of each group or of the group means. The test statistic for this type of situation is:

$$t = \frac{\bar{d}}{s_d / \sqrt{n}},$$

where: $\bar{d} = \dfrac{\Sigma d}{n} = $ the arithmetic mean of paired differences,

$$S_d = \sqrt{\frac{\Sigma\left(d - \bar{d}\right)^2}{n-1}} = \text{the standard deviation of the differences,}$$

$$df = n - 1$$

and n = the number of matched pairs.

The same five step outline as used previously may be followed to solve this type of problem; however, the notations used in stating the hypothesis must reflect that we are testing differences rather than independent means. Therefore, the setups for stating hypotheses are:

1. $H_0: \mu_d = 0$

   $H_1: \mu_d \neq 0$ (2-tailed test)

   This setup is used for testing to determine if the mean difference is significant. No directional difference is implied.

2. $H_0: \mu_d \geq 0$

   $H_1: \mu_d < 0$ (1-tailed test)

   This setup is used if we are interested in determining if the mean difference is less than 0; i.e., if the responses in the first group were significantly less than those of the second group.

3. $H_0: \mu_d \leq 0$

   $H_1: \mu_d > 0$ (1–tailed test)

   This setup is used if we are interested in determining if the mean difference is greater than 0; i.e., if the responses of the first group were significantly greater than those of the second group.

EXAMPLE:

During training, salesmen are paid a fixed salary as opposed to a commission. After the training period, however, salesmen are paid a commission of 3% of total sales volume. The sales manager wishes to determine if the salesmen sell more when they are on commission than they sell when they are being paid a fixed salary. He randomly selects 10 salesmen and compares their sales during training with the equivalent period immediately following the training period. He records the following data:

Salesman	Weekly Sales On Fixed Salary	Weekly Sales On Commission
1	$ 15,625	$14,900
2	12,433	15,630
3	16,812	16,000
4	10,710	12,590
5	14,315	15,000
6	12,500	14,010
7	13,375	15,650
8	15,425	15,400
9	16,000	15,000
10	15,560	16,000

Test at the .05 level to determine if the commission plan results in greater sales.

Step 1. State null and alternative hypotheses.

$H_0: \mu_d \geq 0$

$H_1: \mu_d < 0$ (1-tailed test)

We use this setup because we are interested in determining if the responses in the first case (fixed salary sales) are significantly less than the responses in the second case (commission sales).

Step 2. Specify the values stated in the problem.

Here the values are given as raw data; therefore, we must calculate all the values to use in our calculation. We know that:

n = number of matched pairs = 10, and
$$\alpha = .05.$$

Step 3. Determine the appropriate distribution and a value from the appropriate table.

The Student's t-distribution is used due to the small sample size.

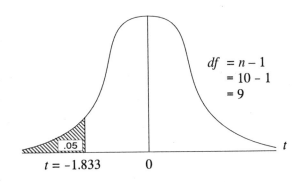

$$df = n - 1$$
$$= 10 - 1$$
$$= 9$$

.05

$t = -1.833$ 0

Therefore, $t* = -1.833$.

Step 4. Compute t.

$$\bar{d} = \frac{\Sigma d}{n} = -7425/10 = -742.5$$

$$S_d = \sqrt{\Sigma(d-\bar{d})^2/n-1} = \sqrt{18,546,290.5/9} = \sqrt{2,060,298.944} = 1,435.5$$

$$t = \frac{\bar{d}}{S_d/\sqrt{n}} = \frac{-742.5}{1,435.5/\sqrt{10}} = \frac{-742.5}{453.95} = -1.636$$

d	$d - \bar{d}$	$(d - \bar{d})^2$
725	1467.5	2,153,556.25
-3197	-2454.5	6,024,570.25
812	1554.5	2,416,470.25
-1880	-1137.5	1,293,906.25
-685	57.5	3,306.25
-1510	-767.5	589,056.25
-2275	-1532.5	2,348,556.25
25	767.5	589,506.25
1000	1742.5	3,036,306.25
-440	302.5	91,506.25
-7425		18,546,290.25

Step 5. Draw a conclusion.

Since -1.636 > -1.833, we should fail to reject the null hypothesis. This implies that these data do not support the sales manager's position that commissioned workers sell more than they do when they are salaried. To further investigate, additional data would need to be gathered. Also, graphically, we can see that the value of -1.636, if placed along the t-axis, will fall outside of the tail of the curve or within the "fail to reject" region.

Note here that we used the t-test due to the fact that our sample was only 10. If the sample size had been 30 or greater, the Z-test would have been used, based on the central limit theorem.

CHAPTER 9

ANALYSIS OF VARIANCE

9.1 ONE-WAY ANALYSIS OF VARIANCE

In Chapter 1, we studied the Student's t-distribution and used it to test the null hypothesis, H_0: $\mu_1 = \mu_2$ (or one of the other versions depending on what we were really interested in testing). Analysis of Variance (ANOVA) is a technique which carries us one step farther; i.e., it allows us to test two or more population means simultaneously. For example, if we have three population means which are being tested, our null hypothesis would be stated as:

$$H_0: \mu_1 = \mu_2 = \mu_3,$$

and this may be extended to cover as many populations as we need to include. The more general approach to use in expressing this null hypothesis is:

$$H_0: \mu_1 = \mu_2 = ... = \mu_k,$$

where k equals the number of population means included in the test.

The term *one-way analysis of variance* is used interchangeably with the term *completely randomized design*. This is a technique used to test for the equality of two or more population means in an experimental design setting. An experimental design is a plan which is established in order to determine the data that must be collected in order to perform a particular experiment. The experiment could pertain to such things as teaching styles, promotional techniques, sales techniques, price variations, or the shelf location of products. This "thing" being studied is referred to as a *factor*. The possible options of the factors which are being investigated (e.g., lecture, case study, and visual aids, if we are studying teaching styles) are the *levels* of the factor and are generally referred to as *treatments*. So, for example, our experimental design might involve testing to determine if sales of a particular item were affected by the approach taken in attempting to sell the item. Possible approaches which might be investigated are door-to-door, telephone, direct mail, and retail. Here, the factor is method of sales of the "item," and the levels or treatments are the four approaches mentioned above.

The term *completely randomized design* is appropriate since the sampling units are randomly assigned to the treatments. The number of sampling units assigned to each treatment or level may be the same or, if the situation calls for it, the number of sampling units may differ from treatment to treatment. The term *one-way analysis of variance*, which we have said is used interchangeably with *completely randomized design*, reflects another characteristic of this particular design. That is, the design allows for studying only one factor. Later we will introduce techniques that allow for simultaneously testing more than one factor.

Even though we are testing mean differences, it is the variance (standard deviation squared) which we will use in performing the tests. This is indicated by the name of the procedure; i.e., analysis of variance. The model for the one-way design is expressed as:

$$X_{ij} = \mu + \tau_j + \varepsilon_{ij}$$

where: X_{ij} = the individual observation *(i)* in group or treatment *(j)*,

μ = a constant value common to every observation,

τ_j(Greek letter tau) = the treatment effect for each group or treatment level *(j)*,

ε_{ij}(Greek letter epsilon) = random error for each observation *(i)* in each treatment group *(j)*.

The assumptions of the model are:

1. Each population is normally distributed;

2. The variances are equal among all populations;

3. The random error terms are independent and normally distributed with a mean of 0 and a standard deviation of σ ; ε_{ij} are NID $(0,\sigma)$.

So, the model for the completely randomized design says that each observation being studied is composed of three parts. One is a constant value common to all; a second is some value that exists due to the effect of the treatment; and finally, there is the random error. The question which the technique attempts to answer is if the outcome associated with the different treatments varies enough to conclude that one treatment affected the value of X_{ij} more than some other treatment did. This involves statistical inference and hypothesis testing.

In the last chapter, we performed hypothesis tests using both the Z-standard normal distribution as well as the Student's t-distribution, depending on which was appropriate for the particular problem. We now introduce still another distribution, the F-distribution, which is applied when testing analysis of variance models. The F-distribution is not symmetrical like the Z and the t; it is skewed to the right and is defined by not one, but two degrees-of-freedom values. One is referred to as the numerator degrees of freedom (v_1) and the other is referred to as the denominator degrees of freedom (v_2). Both must be determined in order to read from an F-Distribution Table. The F-distribution is not represented by one constant distribution as the Z is, but rather changes shapes as does the t-distribution, depending on the number of degrees-of-freedom (v_1, v_2). The general shape of the F-curve is as illustrated below; however, the skewness becomes less and less pronounced as the degrees-of-freedom become larger and larger.

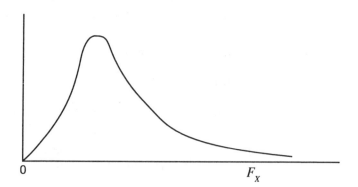

Note that the values of F range from 0 to infinity. Negative values do not exist in the F-distribution.

When testing an analysis of variance problem using the F-test, we typically set up an ANOVA table which assists in calculating the values that will eventually lead us to the determination of the F-statistic. The table for the one-way or completely randomized design is typically set up in the following manner.

ANOVA TABLE

Source of Variation	Sums of Squares	Degrees of Freedom	Mean Square	F
Treatment	SSTR	k-1	MSTR = SSTR/k-1	MSTR/MSE
Error	SSE	N-k	MSE = SSE/N-k	
TOTAL	SST	N-1		

The next question is, how do we determine the value of *SSTR* and *SSE*, and how do we know what values to use for v_1 and v_2? These values are either calculated or determined from equations which take into account the data values that have been randomly assigned to the treatments being studied. The term "sums of squares" is the key in describing the types of calculations required.

SUM OF SQUARES – TREATMENT:

$$SSTR = \sum_{j=1}^{k} n_j \left(\overline{X}_j - \overline{X} \right)^2$$

where: n_j = the number of observations in treatment group j,

k = the number of treatments being studied,

$\overline{X}_j$ = the mean of treatment j,

$\overline{X}$ = the grand mean; i.e., the mean of all observations.

SUM OF SQUARES – ERROR:

$$SSE = \sum_{j=1}^{k} \sum_{i=1}^{n_j} \left(x_{ij} - \overline{x}_j \right)^2$$

where: X_{ij} = observation i in treatment group j.

SUM OF SQUARES – TOTAL:

$$SST = \sum_{j=1}^{k} \sum_{i=1}^{n_j} \left(x_{ij} - \bar{x}\right)^2$$

Computational formulas which are much easier to use are presented below.

$$SSTR = \sum_{j=1}^{k} \frac{T_j^2}{n_j} - \frac{T^2}{n}$$

where: T_j^2 = the square of the sum of all observations in treatment group j.

T^2 = the square of the sum of all observations,

n_j = the number of observations in treatment group j,

N = the total number of all observations.

$$SSE = \sum_{j=1}^{k} \sum_{i=1}^{n_j} X_{ij}^2 - \sum_{j=1}^{k} \frac{T^2}{n_j}$$

where $\sum_{j=1}^{k} \sum_{i=1}^{n_j} X_{ij}^2$ = the sum of all the squared observations in all treatment groups,

$\sum_{j=1}^{k} \frac{T^2}{n_j}$ = same value as previously calculated for the same notation in $SSTR$.

$$SST = \sum_{j=1}^{k} \sum_{i=1}^{n_j} X_{ij}^2 - \frac{T^2}{N}$$

where: $\displaystyle\sum_{j=1}^{k}\sum_{i=1}^{n_j} X_{ij}^2$ = same value as previously calculated for same notation in SSE,

$\dfrac{T^2}{N}$ = same value as previously calculated for same notation in $SSTR$.

An example will serve to bring all of this together. We will see from studying the example that we are still following a basic hypothesis, testing outline, and the five steps from the preceding chapter will be followed.

EXAMPLE:

Three different promotional campaigns are studied in order to determine which is most effective in selling watermelons. The experimental design involved the random assignment of the three different promotional techniques to three comparable grocery stores in a certain city. At the end of one week, daily sales of watermelons were recorded for each of the three stores. These sales figures are presented below:

DAILY SALES OF WATERMELONS

STORE 1	STORE 2	STORE 3
125	50	30
83	75	45
90	80	60
85	100	50
100	40	40
50	60	25
40	50	30
573	455	280
$\overline{X}_1 = 81.9$	$\overline{X}_2 = 65$	$\overline{X}_3 = 40$

Test at the .05 level of significance to determine if a significant difference exists in the mean number of watermelons sold based on the difference in promotional campaigns.

SOLUTION:

Step 1. State the null and alternative hypotheses.

$H_0: \mu_1 = \mu_2 = \mu_3$
$H_1:$ some inequality does exist

The hypothesis setup for ANOVA is always stated as above. The null hypothesis always indicates no difference between group means while the alternative hypothesis simply indicates that some difference does exist. There is no directional alternative hypothesis involved in this test.

Step 2.   State the values specified in the problem.

Usually, in ANOVA problems, the data are given in raw values as with this example. We know that:

$$n_1 = 7; n_2 = 7; n_3 = 7$$
$$\alpha = .05$$

All other values needed must be calculated.

Step 3.   Determine the appropriate distribution and a value from the appropriate table.

The appropriate distribution for an ANOVA problem is the F-distribution. We need to determine a value from the F-table, which requires knowledge of v_1 (numerator degrees of freedom) and v_2 (denominator degrees of freedom).

$$v_1 = k - 1 = 3 - 1 = 2$$
$$v_2 = N - k = 21 - 3 = 18$$

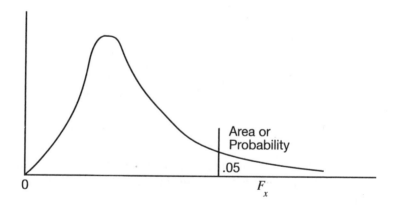

Therefore, $F = 3.16$.

Step 4.   Calculate the value of F.

As we have seen, the calculation of F is somewhat more involved than the calculation of either Z or t. Here we must calculate the values of the sums of squares and use these values to set up the ANOVA table for the determination of the F-value.

We will assume that the assumptions of the model are met; i.e.,

1. Each of the three populations is normally distributed;
2. The three population variances are identical; and,
3. The random error terms are independent and normally distributed with a mean of 0 and a standard deviation of

$$\sigma \; ; \; \varepsilon_{ij} \text{ are } (0, \sigma).$$

The testing of these assumptions is beyond the scope of this presentation; however, these tests may be performed using computer analyses.

DAILY SALES OF WATERMELONS

Store 1	Store 2	Store 3	
$n_1 = 7$	$n_2 = 7$	$n_3 = 7$	$N = 21$
$T_1 = 573$	$T_2 = 455$	$T_3 = 280$	$T = 1308$
$T_1^2 = 328{,}329$	$T_2^2 = 207{,}025$	$T_3^2 = 78{,}400$	$T^2 = 613{,}754$

$$\sum_{j=1}^{3} \sum_{i=1}^{7} X_{ij}^2 = 96{,}314$$

$$SSTR = \sum_{i=1}^{3} \frac{T_j^2}{n_j} - \frac{T^2}{N}$$

$$= \left(328{,}329/7 + 207{,}025/7 + 78{,}400/7\right) - 613{,}754/21$$

$$= \left(46{,}904.14 + 29{,}575 + 11200\right) - 29{,}226.38$$

$$= 87{,}679.14 - 29{,}226.38$$

$$= 5,8452.76$$

$$SSE = \sum_{j=1}^{3} \sum_{k=1}^{7} X_{ij}^2 - \sum_{j=1}^{3} \frac{T^2}{n_j}$$

$$= 96,314 - 87,679.14$$

$$= 8,634.86$$

$$SST = \sum_{j=1}^{3} \sum_{i=1}^{7} X_{ij}^2 - \frac{T^2}{N}$$

$$= 96,314 - 29,226.38$$

$$= 67,087.62.$$

ANOVA TABLE

Source of Variation	Sums of Squares	Degrees of Freedom	Mean Square	F-value
Treatment	58,452.76	2	29,226.38	60.92
Error	8,634.86	18	479.71	
TOTAL	67,087.62	20		

Step 5.   Since 60.92 > 3.16, we reject the null hypothesis (H_0:) and accept the alternative hypothesis (H_1:). This is an indication that the mean number of watermelons sold does differ among stores; i.e., among different promotional techniques. However, we cannot conclude where the differences lie. By observation, we see that Store A's average sales was the largest and Store B's was greater than Store C's. However, simple observation does not allow us to conclude where true significant differences lie. In order to determine that, we must use still another procedure which will be discussed later in this chapter. Recall, also, that we do have a 5% chance that our decision is in error.

9.2 RANDOMIZED BLOCK DESIGN

The randomized block design involves extending the completely randomized design by adding an additional term to the model. The term (or factor) which is added is referred to as a **blocking** factor and allows for reducing the overall error term when the blocking factor is a significant variable. This experimental design calls for grouping the units being studied into homogeneous groups or blocks and then randomly assigning treatments to the units. As an illustration, let's assume that we are interested in testing three different teaching methods, but that we realize that time-of-day when the classes are taught is a factor which might influence the outcome of the test results. Therefore, the randomized block design would allow us to test for a mean difference between test scores for the three different teaching methods, while controlling for (or blocking on) time-of-day, by randomly assigning one student to each treatment/block combination. The model for the randomized block design is:

$$X_{ij} = \mu + \beta_i + \tau_j + \varepsilon_{ij}$$

where: X_{ij} = the individual observation *(i)* in group or treatment *(j)*,

μ = a constant value common to every observation,

β_i (Greek letter beta) = the blocking effect of block *(i)*,

τ_j (Greek letter tau) = the treatment effect for each group or treatment level *(j)*,

ε_{ij} (Greek letter epsilon) = random error for each observation in block *(i)* and treatment group *(j)*.

The assumptions of the model are:

1. Each population is normally distributed;
2. The variances are equal among all populations;
3. Only one observation is assigned to each block/treatment combination;
4. The blocking effect and the treatment effects do not interact; i.e., the treatment effect is the same over all blocks;

5. The error terms are independent and normally distributed with a mean of zero; i.e., ε_{ij} are NID $(0, \sigma)$. That is the random error terms are independent and normally distributed with a mean of 0 and a standard deviation of σ; ε_{ij} are $(0, \sigma)$.

We approach the solution to a randomized block design problem very much like we solved the completely randomized design. We must calculate sums of squares and use these values in the ANOVA table in conjunction with degrees-of-freedom values in order to arrive at a value for F. The difference here is that we must now allocate space in the table for the blocking effect; therefore, our ANOVA table will take the following form.

ANOVA TABLE

Source of Variation	Sums of Squares	Degrees of Freedom	Mean Squares	F-Value
Treatment	SSTR	$k-1$	MSTR=SSTR/k-1	MSTR/MSE
Block	SSB	$b-1$	MSB=SSB/b-1	MSB/MSE
Error	SSE	$(k-1)(b-1)$	MSE=SSE(k-1)(b-1)	
TOTAL	SST	N-1		

Note here that this table yields two F-values, one for testing the effect of treatments and the other for testing the effect of blocking. Whereas we are truly only interested in testing treatment differences, it is worthwhile to observe the outcome of the blocking factor as well. If the F-value for the blocking effect is not significant, this implies that the experiment is poorly designed and that we did not accomplish anything by using the randomized block design over the completely randomized design.

The equations for the sums of squares, in their computational forms, are:

$$SSTR = \frac{\sum_{j=1}^{k} T_j^2}{k} - \frac{T^2}{N}$$

where: T_j^2 = the square of the sum of all observations in each treatment group (j),

k = the number of treatment groups,

T^2 = the square of the sum of all observations,

N = the total number of all observations.

136

$$SSB = \frac{\sum\limits_{i=1}^{b} T_i^2}{b} - \frac{T^2}{N}$$

where: T_i^2 = the square of the sum of all observations in block (i),

  b = the number of blocks.

$$SST = \sum_{j=1}^{k} \sum_{i=1}^{n_j} X_{ij}^2 - \frac{T^2}{N}$$

where: $\sum\limits_{j=1}^{k} \sum\limits_{i=1}^{n_j} X_{ij}^2$ = the sum of all squared observations.

$$SSE = SST - SSTR - SSB$$

EXAMPLE:

A manufacturing firm is considering purchasing new equipment. In order to determine which machine to purchase, the manager selects three machines designed to perform the same function from three different manufacturers. He compares the machines in order to determine if there is a significant difference between the number of items that can be produced in one week. There are three operators who work on this type machine and he realizes that there may be some variation that can be attributed to the particular person who is operating the machine. Therefore, he decides on a randomized block design in which each of the three operators works at each of the three machines for one week. The data shown in the table below represents the number of items produced per week for each operator. Test at the .05 level of significance in order to determine if there is a significant treatment effect.

MACHINE
(Number of Items Produced)

OPERATOR		1	2	3		
	1.	45	60	30	$T_1 = 135$	$T_1^2 = 18,225$
	2.	60	70	55	$T_2 = 185$	$T_2^2 = 34,225$
	3.	45	65	40	$T_3 = 150$	$T_3^2 = 22,500$
		$T_1 = 150$	$T_2 = 195$	$T_3 = 125$	$T = 470$	
		$T_1^2 = 22,500$	$T_2^2 = 38,025$	$T_3^2 = 15,625$	$T^2 = 220,900$	
					$N = 9$	

SOLUTION:

Step 1. $H_0: \mu_1 = \mu_2 = \mu_3$
H_1: Some inequality does exist

Step 2. $k = 3$ $\alpha = .05$
$b = 3$
$N = 9$

(NOTE: Steps 3 and 4 are reversed in this example which is usually the case when using the F-test).

Step 3. (See original table for summation.)

$$SSTR = \frac{\sum\limits_{j=1}^{k} T_j^2}{k} - \frac{T^2}{N}$$

$$= \frac{(22{,}500 + 38{,}025 + 15{,}625)}{3} - \frac{220{,}900}{9}$$

$$= \frac{25{,}383.3 - 24{,}544.4}{838.9}$$

$$SSB = \frac{\sum\limits_{i=1}^{b} T_i^2}{b} - \frac{T^2}{N},$$

$$= \frac{(18{,}2255 + 34{,}225 + 22{,}500)}{3} - \frac{220{,}900}{9}$$

$$= 24{,}983.3 - 24{,}544.4$$

$$= 438.9$$

$$SST = \sum\limits_{j=1}^{k} \sum\limits_{i=1}^{n_j} X_{ij}^2 - \frac{T^2}{N}$$

$$= 25{,}900 - 24{,}544.4$$

$$SSE = 1{,}355.6$$

$$SSE = SST - SSTR - SSB$$

$$= 1{,}355.6 - 838.9 - 438.9$$

$$= 77.8.$$

ANOVA TABLE

Source of Variation	Sums of Squares	df	Mean Squares	F-Value
Treatment	838.9	2	419.45	21.57
Block	438.9	2	219.45	11.28
Error	<u>77.8</u>	<u>4</u>	19.45	
TOTAL	1355.6	8		

Step 4.

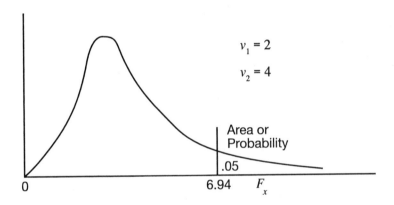

$v_1 = 2$

$v_2 = 4$

Area or Probability

.05

0   6.94 F_x

Therefore, $F = 6.94$.

Step 5.

a) Since $21.57 > 6.94$, we reject H_0: and accept H_1: which indicates that there is a significant difference between the performance of the machines. Again, at this point, we cannot conclude where the differences lie. Also, remember that there is a 5% chance that we have arrived at an incorrect conclusion.

b) Even though the purpose of the experiment was not to test for a difference in the performance of the operators (the blocking effect), we can perform this test. Since $11.28 > 6.94$, we would conclude, with a 5% chance of error, that the operators perform differently. This supports the use of the randomized block design.

9.3 FACTORIAL DESIGNS

Factorial experimental designs allow for the testing of two or more factors simultaneously, as well as all possible interactions. These tests differ from the randomized block design previously discussed in that we are interested in testing all variables involved and we do not assume that one treatment effect is the same over all levels of the other treatment effects. We allow for differences which imply that the treatment effects are possibly working together to explain some of the variations in the data. Neither are we confined to only one observation per treatment level as with the randomized block design.

The model illustrated will include the simplest possible setup which is that of only two factors. It is understood that this model may be extended to cover any number of factors which might be relevant for a given problem.

$$X_{ijc} = \mu + \tau_i + \tau_j + \tau_i\tau_j + \varepsilon_{ijc}$$

where: X_{ijc} = the individual observations (c) in treatment groups i and j,

μ = a constant value common to every observation,

τ_i = effect of ith level of first factor,

τ_j = effect of jth level of second factor,

$\tau_i\tau_j$ = interaction effect of the two treatments combined,

ε_{ijc} = random error for each observation.

The assumptions for the factorial design are even more involved and more difficult to check than are those for the completely randomized design or the randomized block design. They include:

1. Observations in each cell follow a normal distribution;
2. Equal cell variances;
3. Independent and normally distributed error terms; i.e., ε_{ijc} are NID $(0, \sigma)$.

ANOVA TABLE

Source of Variation	Sums of Squares	Degrees of Freedom	Mean Squares	F-Values
Treatment i	$SSTR_i$	$k_i\text{-}1$	$MSTR_i = SSTR_i/k\text{-}1_i$	$MSTR_i/MSE$
Treatment j	$SSTR_j$	$k_j\text{-}1$	$MSTR_j = SSTR_j/k_j$	$MSTR_j/MSE$
Interaction of Treatment	$SSTR_iTR_j$	$(k_i\text{-}1)(k_j\text{-}1)$	$MSTR_iTR_j{=}SSTR_iTR_j/$ $(k_i\text{-}1)(k_j\text{-}1)$	$MSTR_iTR_j/MSE$
Error	SSE	$N - k_ik_j$	$MSE = SSE/N - k_ik_j$	
TOTAL	SST	$N - 1$		

As this ANOVA table illustrates, three F-values are calculated, one for use in testing each of the two main treatment effects and one for the interaction effect. *It is important to note that all interaction effects are tested first. If any are significant at the specified level of significance, the treatment effects involved in the significant interaction are not tested; however, if none of the interaction effects are significant, all main effects are then tested.* The explanation of the theory behind this rule is beyond the level of the material presented herein. As the number of treatment effects being tested increases, the ANOVA table is expanded to include all treatment effects as well as all possible interaction effects resulting from these treatments.

The equations for the sums of squares, in their computational forms, are:

$$SSTR_i = \frac{\sum_{i=1}^{k_i} T_i^2}{nk_i} - \frac{T^2}{N}$$

where: T_i^2 = the square of the sum of all observations in treatment i level,

n = number of observations in level of treatment i,

k_i = number of treatment i levels,

T^2 = the square of the sum of all observations,

N = total number of all observations.

$$SSTR_j = \frac{\sum_{j=1} T_j^2}{nk_j} - \frac{T^2}{N}$$

where: T_j^2 = the square of the sum of all observations in treatment j level,

n = number of observations in level of treatment j,

k_j = number of treatment j levels.

$$SSE = \sum_i \sum_j \sum_c X_{ijc}^2 = \frac{\sum_i \sum_j T_{ij}^2}{n}$$

where: $\sum_i \sum_j \sum_c X_{ijc}^2$ = the sum of the square of all observations,

$\sum_i \sum_j T_{ij}^2$ = the sum of the square of all observations for treatment i and treatment j.

$$SST = \sum_i \sum_j \sum_c X_{ijc}^2 - \frac{T^2}{N}$$

$$SSTR_iTR_j = SST - SSTR_i - SSTR_j - SSE$$

EXAMPLE:

In analyzing the sales of a product, a store manager looked at the price of the product in conjunction with a display location within the store. He collected the following sales data for his experimental design.

UNITS SOLD
Price (j)

		$1.25/unit	$1.50/unit	$2.00/unit
	Outside	50 45	45 45	30 36
LOCATION (i)	Inside-Front	40 30	30 20	20 21
	Inside-Rear	35 20	20 16	25 15

Test to determine if location or price or a combination of the price and location (interaction effect) plays a significant role in sales differential. Perform these tests at the .05 level of significance.

SOLUTION:

Step 1. a) H_0: There is no significant interaction effect when combining price and display location.

H_1: There is a significant interaction effect.

If we fail to conclude that a significant interaction exists, then we test:

b) H_0: $\mu_1 = \mu_2 = \mu_3$ for location
H_1: some inequality does exist

c) H_0: $\mu_1 = \mu_2 = \mu_3$ for price
H_1: some inequality does exist

Step 2. $k_i = 3$ $\qquad\qquad\qquad\qquad$ $k_j = 3$

$$n_{ij} = 2$$
$$N = 18$$
$$\alpha = .05$$

143

Step 3.

		Price (j)			
		$1.25/unit	$1.50/unit	$2.00/unit	
LOCATION (i)	Outside	$T_{11}^2 = 9025$	$T_{12}^2 = 8100$	$T_{13}^2 = 4356$	
	Inside-Front	$T_{21}^2 = 4900$	$T_{22}^2 = 2500$	$T_{23}^2 = 1681$	
	Inside-Rear	$T_{31}^2 = 3025$	$T_{32}^2 = 1296$	$T_{33}^2 = 1600$	

$T_{1.} = 251$

$T_{1.}^2 = 63001$

$T_{2.} = 161$

$T_{2.}^2 = 25921$

$T_{3.} = 131$

$T_{3.}^2 = 17161$

$T = 543$

$T^2 = 294,849$

$T_{.1} = 220 \qquad T_{.2} = 176 \qquad T_{.3} = 147$

$T_{.1}^2 = 48400 \qquad T_{.2}^2 = 30976 \qquad T_{.3}^2 = 21609$

$$SSTR_i = \frac{\Sigma T_i^2}{nk_i} = \frac{T^2}{N}$$

$$= \frac{63001 = 25921 + 17161}{2(3)} - \frac{294,849}{18}$$

$$= 17680.5 - 16,380.5$$

$$= 1300$$

$$SSTR_j = \frac{ST_j^2}{n_{kj}} - \frac{T^2}{N}$$

$$= \frac{48400 + 30976 + 21609}{2(3)} - 16,380.5$$

$$= 16830.8 - 16380.5$$

$$= 450.3$$

$$SSE = \Sigma_i \ \Sigma_j \ \Sigma_c \ X_{ijc}^2 \ - \ \frac{\Sigma_i \Sigma_j \ T_{ij}^2}{n}$$

$$= \ 18{,}543 \ - \ \frac{36483}{2}$$

$$= \ 18{,}543 \ - \ 18241.5$$

$$= \ 301.5$$

$$SST \ = \ \Sigma_i \ \Sigma_j \ \Sigma_c \ X_{ijc}^2 \ - \ \frac{T^2}{N}$$

$$= \ 18{,}543 \ - \ 16{,}380.5$$

$$= \ 2162.5$$

$$SSTRP_iTR_j \ = \ SST - SSTR_i \ - \ SSTR_j \ - \ SSE$$

$$= \ 2162.5 \ - \ 1300 \ - \ 450.3 \ - \ 301.5$$

$$= \ 110.7$$

ANOVA TABLE

Source of Variation	Sums of Squares	Degrees of Freedom	Mean Squares	F-Values
Location	1300.0	2	650.0	19.40
Price	450.3	2	225.2	6.72
Loc X Price	110.7	4	27.7	.83
Error	<u>301.5</u>	<u>9</u>	33.5	
TOTAL	2162.5	17		

Step 4. a) For testing interaction effect,
$$v_1 = 4$$
$$v_2 = 9.$$

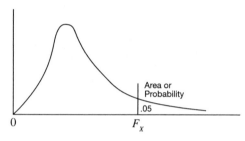

Therefore, $F = 3.6331.$

b) For testing main effects,

$$v_1 = 2$$

$$v_2 = 9.$$

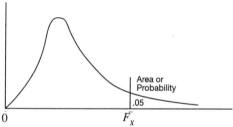

Therefore, $F = 4.2565.$

Step 5. a) **Interaction Effect**
Since $.83 < 3.6331$, we fail to reject H_0:, which is an indication that we cannot conclude that a significant interaction exists when looking at price and display location jointly. Therefore, we may continue on to test the main effects.

b) **Location Main Effect**
Since $19.4 > 4.2565$, we reject the null hypothesis and accept the alternative which concludes that a significant difference does exist in sales for the different locations. At this time, we cannot say specifically where the differ-

ences lie; we also have a 5% chance of having reached an erroneous conclusion.

c) **Price Main Effect**
Since 6.72 > 4.2565, we reject the null hypothesis and accept the alternative hypothesis that sales differ based on price. Again, we cannot yet conclude where the differences are and we have a 5% chance that our conclusion is in error.

9.4 MULTIPLE COMPARISONS TESTS

Analysis of variance, as we have seen, is a technique for comparing two or more means in order to determine if they are significantly different from each other. We have seen in some of our examples that the F-statistic was large enough to allow us to reject a null hypothesis (H_0: $\mu_1 = \mu_2 = \mu_3 = \ldots = \mu_k$) in favor of the alternative hypothesis (H_1: some inequality does exist). The question that we are then faced with is, "Where does the difference lie?" That is, are all of the means being tested significantly different from each other or are only some significantly different? For example, if we are testing three population means and we determine that a significant difference exists using ANOVA, the possible differences which we must compare are:

$$\mu_1 \text{ and } \mu_2$$
$$\mu_1 \text{ and } \mu_3$$
$$\mu_2 \text{ and } \mu_3.$$

By using some form of a multiple comparison test, we are able to determine where, in these three possible pairings, the significant differences lie. This is valuable information allowing us to make important business decisions. Note that as the number of means being tested increases by one, the number of pairwise comparisons increases exponentially. That is, k means would yield

$$\binom{k}{2} = \frac{k!}{2!(k-2)!} = \frac{(k)(k-1)}{2} \text{ pairwise comparisons.}$$

The procedures for performing multiple comparisons tests are not generally included at this level and are usually performed, as are analysis of variance procedures, using the computer. Some of the more common multiple comparisons tests are Fisher's LSD, Tuhey's method, Duncan's method, Scheffé's method, and Linear Contrasts.

CHAPTER 10

SIMPLE LINEAR REGRESSION

10.1 SCATTER DIAGRAM

A *scatter diagram* is a graphic representation of the relationship between two variables. It consists of an X-axis for coding the *independent variable* and a Y-axis for coding the *dependent variable*. The data values are represented by points or dots within the grid and are plotted as they relate to both the X and Y variables.

EXAMPLE:

X = Speed of Machine (rpm)	Y = % Defectives Produced by Machine
50	1.5
75	1.9
60	2.0
65	1.5
90	3.0
70	2.5
55	1.0
45	1.2
80	1.7
70	2.0

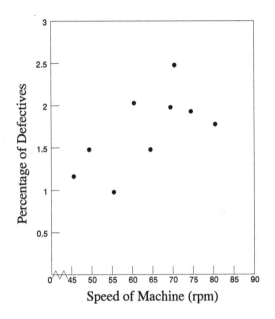

Speed of Machine (rpm)

The purpose of a scatter diagram is to allow for the comparison of the independent variable (X) with the dependent variable (Y) so that we may get a feel for how they are related. We can observe both the direction of the relationship, i.e., whether they are both changing in the same direction or in opposite directions, as well as the apparent strength of the relationship between the two variables. If we imagine a straight line through the middle of the points and then look at how close the points are to this imaginary line, we can get some idea about the strength of the relationship. The closer the points are to the line, and the sharper the slope of the line, the stronger the relationship between X and Y.

10.2 REGRESSION EQUATION

Simple linear regression is a technique by which one dependent variable (Y) is regressed against one independent variable (X) and the relationship between the two is in the form of a straight line. The equation for calculation of the regression line is:

$$Y_i = a + bX_i$$

where: Y_i = the ith value of the dependent variable,

X_i = the ith value of the independent variable.

149

$$b = \frac{\Sigma XY - n\overline{X}\overline{Y}}{\Sigma X^2 - n\overline{X}^2}$$

$$a = \frac{\Sigma Y - b\Sigma X}{n}$$

EXAMPLE:

Assume that we use the data from the previous example and compute the regression equation where X = speed of machine measured in revolutions per minute and Y = percentage of defective items produced by the machine at the specified rates.

X (rpm)	Y (%)	XY	X^2
50	1.5	75.0	2,500
75	1.9	142.5	5,625
60	2.0	120.0	3,600
65	1.5	97.5	4,225
90	3.0	270.0	8,100
70	2.5	175.0	4,900
55	1.0	55.0	3,025
45	1.2	54.0	2,025
80	1.7	136.0	6,400
70	2.0	140.0	4,900
TOTAL 660	18.3	1,265.0	45,300

$$\overline{X} = \Sigma X/n$$
$$= 660/10$$
$$= 66$$

$$\overline{Y} = \Sigma Y/n$$
$$= 18.3/10$$
$$= 1.83$$

$$b = \frac{\Sigma XY - n\overline{X}\,\overline{Y}}{\Sigma X^2 - n\overline{X}^2}$$

$$= \frac{1265 - 10(66)(1.83)}{45,300 - 10(66)^2}$$

$$= \frac{1265 - 1207.8}{45,300 - 43,560}$$

$$= \frac{57.2}{1740}$$

$$= .033$$

$$a = \frac{\Sigma Y - b\,\Sigma X}{n}$$

$$= \frac{18.3 - .033(660)}{10}$$

$$= \frac{18.3 - 21.78}{10}$$

$$= \frac{-3.48}{10}$$

$$= -.348$$

Therefore: $Y = a + bX$, i.e.,

$$Y = -.348 + .033X.$$

The value of "b" is the slope of the line. In this equation, $b = .033$ tells us that for every unit increase in rpm, the percentage of defective units produced increases by .033 percent. This is an indication of a positive relationship between X and Y; i.e., as X increases, Y also increases, as evident as well from the scatter diagram. The value of "a," which is the y-intercept, indicates that at the point where X = 0, the regression line

SCATTER DIAGRAM
WITH REGRESSION LINE

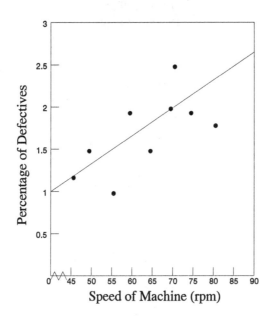

crosses the Y-axis at -.348. A strict interpretation of this value would be that if we operate the machine at 0 rpm, we would produce -.348% defectives. Obviously, if we were operating the machine at 0 rpm, it would not be producing any items and, consequently, the percentage of defectives would be 0 also. We must keep in mind that the regression equation is valid only for a relevant range of X values. Two possible modifications (which are beyond the scope of this text) which would resolve this problem are regression through the origin, and (even better) logistic regression.

Once we have plotted the data in a scatter diagram and calculated the regression equation, it is generally useful to plot a regression line. Since we know that this will be a straight line, we may substitute two values for X into the equation, solve for Y, and plot the straight line from these points. Using the previous example, we can illustrate this.

152

EXAMPLE:

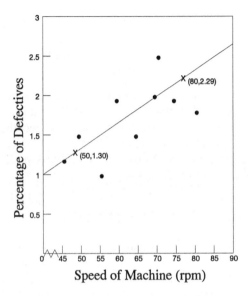

Speed of Machine (rpm)

If $X = 50$; $Y = -.348 + .033(50)$ If $X = 80$; $Y = -.348 + .033(80)$
$ = 1.30$ $= 2.29$

Now we have a "real" line through the data points and we can observe that the points fall "relatively" close to the line, which implies that the relationship between the speed at which the machine operates and the percentage of defectives it produces is "relatively" strong. Also, we note that the relationship is positive in that the line has an upward slope. If the relationship is inverse or negative, the sign of "b" will be negative and the regression line will therefore slope downward.

Once we have measured the relationship between X and Y, of what value is this knowledge? If we are satisfied that the relationship is strong enough, we may use the regression equation X to predict the value of Y from predetermined values of X. For example, what percentages of defective items should we expect if we set the rpm rate at some prespecified value? We can answer this question by substituting this prespecified value into the equation for X and solving for Y.

EXAMPLE:

What percentage of defectives would we expect if we set the rpm rate at 95?

$$Y = a + bX$$
$$Y = -.348 + .033(95)$$
$$Y = 2.787 \text{ or } 2.79\%$$

What percentage of defectives would we expect if we set the rpm rate at 40?

$$Y = -.348 + .033(40)$$
$$= .972 \text{ or } .97\%$$

Note that when we use a regression equation to predict values of Y from X, we should not use X values that are extremely different from those which were used to build the equation. That is, we cannot expect the same linear relationship to hold indefinitely over all values of X. Also, we must be sure when predicting that the assumptions of the regression model (which will be discussed in section 3.4) are met.

10.3 PREDICTION ACCURACY

When we use a regression equation to predict values of Y from pre-specified values of X, it is important to be able to determine the accuracy of the prediction. A measure exists which allows us to measure accuracy and it might be thought of as a comparable measure to the standard deviation which serves to measure the "accuracy" of the mean. This accuracy measure is termed the *standard error of the estimate,* and it measures the average vertical distance between the data points and the regression line. The formula for this measure is:

$$S_{y \cdot x} = \sqrt{\frac{\Sigma \left(Y - \hat{Y} \right)^2}{n - 2}}$$

where: $S_{y \cdot x}$ = notation for the standard error of the estimate,

$\hat{Y}$ = the predicted values of Y from the regression equation corresponding to the X observations,

Y = observed values of Y,

n = number of (X,Y) data pairs.

A computational formula which is easier to solve is:

$$S_{y \cdot x} = \sqrt{\frac{\Sigma Y^2 - a\Sigma Y - b\Sigma XY}{n-2}}$$

EXAMPLE:

Using the same data set, we can solve for $S_{y \cdot x}$ using values previously determined. We will, however, have to determine the value of the ΣY^2, since it was not required in the earlier calculations. We square each of the Y values and sum, as shown below.

Y	Y^2
.5	2.25
1.9	3.61
2.0	4.00
.5	2.25
3.0	9.00
2.5	6.25
1.0	1.00
1.2	1.44
1.7	2.89
2.0	4.00
18.3	36.69

$$S_{y \cdot x} = \sqrt{\frac{36.69 - (-.348)(18.3) - (.033)(1265)}{10-2}}$$

$$= \sqrt{\frac{36.69 + 6.3684 - 41.745}{8}}$$

$$= \sqrt{\frac{1.3134}{8}}$$

$$= \sqrt{.164175}$$

$$= .405\% \quad \text{(Note that } S_{y \cdot x} \text{ is always in the unit of the } Y \text{ variable.)}$$

155

This indicates that the average vertical distance between the data points and the regression line is .405%. The smaller this value, the closer the points fall to the line and the more accurate is the prediction.

The interpretation of the size of the value, however, is at this point rather arbitrary. That is, we cannot say definitely that .405% is small, but we can begin to get a general feel for its relative size by observing the scatter diagram. Since this shows that the points fall relatively close to the line, we will tend to conclude, until we have additional information, that .405% is relatively small and, consequently, we can make relatively accurate predictions of the percentage of defectives from the rpm setting of the machine.

SCATTER DIAGRAM ILLUSTRATING THE CALCULATION OF $S_{y\cdot x}$

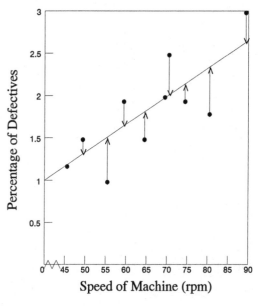

Each vertical line reflects the distance between a data point and the regression line ($Y_i - \hat{Y}$)

10.4 REGRESSION MODEL AND HYPOTHESIS TESTING

As long as we are simply interested in the relationship between X and Y and we are not interested in drawing conclusions beyond the set of data being analyzed, we may perform the calculations for the regression equation as we have just illustrated. However, if the data being analyzed represent a random sample and we desire to infer our results to the population from which the sample was drawn, we must look at regression analysis in its inferential sense and describe the model and the supporting assumptions.

The simple linear regression model is:

$$Y_i = \alpha + \beta X_i + \varepsilon_i$$

where: Y_i = individual values of the dependent variable,

X_i = individual values of the independent variable,

α = the y-intercept or the value of Y where $X = 0$

β = the slope of the line or the change in Y per unit change in X,

ε_i = error term for each value of Y.

The assumptions of the model are:

1. X is a non-random predetermined measure.
2. For any given value of X, there exist many values of Y which are normally distributed with equal variances over all Xs.
3. Y is a random variable and the individual values of Y (given X) are statistically independent.
4. Therefore, since ε_i = the difference between Y and $\hat{Y}$, ε_i is NID (O, σ^2).

When these conditions are met, we may use regression analysis as an inferential tool and apply both confidence interval estimates and hypothesis testing. Although these techniques may be applied to both the intercept (α) and the slope (β), the real interpretative interest lies in the slope of the equation since it tells us the direction and the strength of the relationship between the two variables. Therefore, we will confine our discussion of confidence interval estimates and hypothesis testing to the slope (β).

Confidence Interval Estimates for the Slope

We illustrated in *Essentials of Business Statistics I*, and in Chapter 1 of this volume, the notion of hypothesis testing and the role of the Z-distribution and the Student's *t*-distribution. The same theory applies here; however, we must apply the correct equations as we work through our steps in the problem-solving process. In order to calculate the confidence interval to estimate the slope of the line in the population, we use the following equation:

$$Pr[b - t_{(\alpha/2, df)} S_b \le \beta \le b + t_{(\alpha/2, df)} S_b] = (1 - \alpha) \, 1$$

where: b = slope of the line for the sample,
$t_{(\alpha/2, df)}$ = value from the Student's t-distribution with $df = n - 2$
α = level of significance (1 - confidence coefficient)

$$S_b = \frac{S_{y \cdot x}}{\sqrt{\Sigma X^2 - \frac{(\Sigma X)^2}{N}}}$$

EXAMPLE:

Let's assume that the 10 observations previously used represent a random sample and that all of the assumptions of the regression model are met. Produce a 95% confidence interval estimate of β, the slope of the line, for the population regression equation.

SOLUTION:

Y = $-.348 + .033X$; $S_{y \cdot x}$ = $.405$
b = $.033$
t = $(.05/2, df = 10\text{-}2) \pm 2.306$

$$S_b = \frac{.405}{\sqrt{45,300 - \frac{(660)^2}{10}}}$$

$$= \frac{.405}{\sqrt{45,300 - 42,560}}$$

$$= \frac{.405}{\sqrt{1740}}$$

$$= \frac{.405}{41.71}$$

$$= .0097.$$

Therefore:

Pr [.033 - (2.306)(.0097) $\leq \beta \leq$ .033 + (2.306)(.0097)] = .95
Pr (.033 - .022 $\leq \beta \leq$ .033 + .022) = .95
Pr (.011 $\leq \beta \leq$ .055) = .95.

We can be 95% confident that the slope of the population regression equation is contained within the range between .011% and .055%. That is, the average percentage increase of defectives for the population per unit increase in rpm is contained within this range, with a 95% certainty.

Confidence Interval Estimates for Prediction

1. Predicting an Average Value of Y for Some Given Value of X

We illustrated earlier that we may use a regression equation to predict Y from predetermined values of X. We also illustrated that we can determine the accuracy of the prediction by calculating a measure called the standard error of the estimate $(S_{y \cdot x})$. Now, we can take this one step farther and construct a confidence interval to predict, with some specified degree of accuracy, the *average* value of Y in the population for a given value of X. The equation for this confidence interval estimate is:

$$\text{Pr} \, [\hat{y} - t_{(\alpha/2, df)} S_{\hat{y} \cdot x} \leq \hat{y} \leq \hat{y} + t_{(\alpha/2, df)} S_{\hat{y} \cdot x}] \, = \, (1 - \alpha) \, 100$$

where: $\hat{Y} = a + bX$ (for some specified value of X),

$$S_{\hat{y} \cdot x} = S_{y \cdot x} \sqrt{1 + \frac{1}{n} + \frac{\left(X - \overline{X}\right)^2}{\sum X^2 \frac{\left(\sum X\right)^2}{n}}} \,,$$

and $S_{y \cdot x}$ = standard error of the estimate.

EXAMPLE:

Assume that we wish to make a 95% confidence interval estimate of Y (the percentage of defective items produced) in the population if we set the speed of the machine at 95 rpm.

SOLUTION:

$$\hat{Y} = -.348+.033(95)$$

$$= 2.79\%$$

$$t_{(.05/2,\ df\ =\ 10-2)} = 2.306$$

$$S_{y\cdot x} = .405\% \qquad\qquad \Sigma X^2 = 45300$$

$$X = 95 \qquad\qquad \Sigma X = 660$$

$$\overline{X} = 66 \qquad\qquad n = 10$$

$$S_{y\cdot x} = .405\sqrt{\frac{1}{10}+\frac{(95-66)^2}{45300-\frac{(660)^2}{10}}} = .309$$

Pr $[2.79 - 2.306(.309) \leq Y \leq 2.79 + .2.306(.309)] = .95$

Pr $(2.79 - .714 \leq Y \leq 2.79 + .714) = .95$

Pr $(2.076 \leq Y \leq 3.504) = .95$

Therefore, we can be 95% confident that the average percentage defective in the population when operating the machine at 95 rpm is contained within the range between 2.076% and 3.504%.

2. Predicting a Single Value of Y for Some Given Value of X

In the preceding example, we calculated a confidence interval to estimate the *average* percentage of defectives in the population of all machines of this particular type. This section will include the procedure for calculating the confidence interval to estimate the percentage defectives *for one particular machine*, once a value of X has been specified. The procedure is very similar to that just explained. However, we extend the limits of the interval on each side of the inequality, making the estimate less precise than that in the previous situation. This is due to the fact that we are estimating a *single value*, which is more difficult to do than to estimate an average.

This confidence interval equation is:

$$\Pr = \left[\hat{y} - t_{(\alpha/2,df)}S_{\hat{y}\times x} \leq y \leq t_{(\alpha/2,df)}S_{y\times x}\right] = (1-\alpha)100$$

where: $y = a + bx$ for some specified value of X,

$$S_{\hat{y} \cdot x} = S_{y \cdot x}\sqrt{1 + \frac{1}{n} + \frac{(X - \bar{X})^2}{\sum X^2 \frac{(\sum X)^2}{n}}}$$

and $S_{y \cdot x}$ = standard error of the estimate.

EXAMPLE:

Assume that we wish to make a 95% confidence interval estimate of the percentage of defectives produced from a single machine if the speed is set at 95 rpm.

SOLUTION:

$\hat{Y}$	= 2.79%	$\sum X^2$	= 45300
t	= 2.306	$\sum X$	= 660
$S_{y \cdot x}$	= .405%	n	= 10
X	= 95		
$\bar{X}$	= 66		

$$S_{\hat{y} \cdot x} = .405\sqrt{1 + \frac{1}{10} + \frac{(95 - 66)^2}{45300 - \frac{(660)^2}{10}}} = .51$$

$$\Pr [2.79 - (2.306)(.51) \leq Y \leq 2.79 + (2.306)(.51)] = .95$$
$$\Pr (2.79 - 1.176 \leq Y \leq 2.79 + 1.176) = .95$$
$$\Pr (1.614 \leq Y \leq 3.966) = .95$$

Therefore, we can be 95% confident that the percentage of defectives from this one machine operating at a speed of 95 rpm, is contained within the range between 1.164% and 3.966%.

Hypothesis Testing

Hypothesis testing in regression analysis is performed in a manner similar to that previously discussed in Chapter 1. Even though the equations are different to reflect the value being tested, the same five step solution process may be applied. We will discuss the testing of a significant β and apply the t-test in the solution.

EXAMPLE:

From the same example problem, let's test to determine if the slope of the equation in the population (β) is significant. That is, is the value of β significantly different from 0 at the .05 level of significance?

SOLUTION:

1. H_0: $\beta = 0$

   H_1: $\beta \neq 0$ (2-tailed test)

This setup allows us to test to determine if the population slope is significantly different from 0. We use this expression because a slope of 0 would yield a horizontal regression line which would indicate absolutely no relationship between X and Y.

2. $n = 10$

   $b = .033$

   $S_b = .0097$

3.

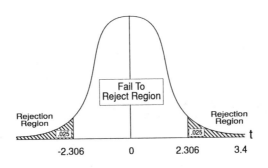

Therefore, $t = \pm 2.306$.

4.

$$t = \frac{b}{S_b}$$

$$= \frac{.033}{.0097}$$

$$= 3.40$$

5. Since $|3.40| > |\pm 2.306|$, we must reject H_0: and accept H_1:, which indicates that $\beta \neq 0$. Therefore, we conclude that the relationship between speed of machine (X) and percentage of defectives (Y) is significant in the population. However, there is a 5% chance that our conclusion is in error, i.e., that we have committed a Type I error.

We should note that there might be occasions when one wants to test for a significant *positive* or *negative* slope. When this is the case, we would state the alternative hypothesis to reflect the appropriate direction while leaving the null hypothesis as stated in this example.

CHAPTER 11

CORRELATION ANALYSIS

11.1 VARIABLE RELATIONSHIPS

In Chapter 3, we illustrated the scatter diagram as a means of plotting one variable against a second so that their relationship might be analyzed. We indicated that a comparison of the data points with the average linear relationship (regression line) will allow us to determine, to some extent, the strength of the relationship. The closer the points fall to the line and the sharper the slope of the line, the stronger is the linear relationship between the two variables. We also noted that the relationship may be either positive (direct) or negative (inverse).

In addition to the linear (straight-line) relationship which we have previously discussed, relationships may also be curvilinear. However, we will not discuss these relative to the calculation of regression equations, etc. Scatter diagrams depicting various types of relationships between X (independent variable) and Y (dependent variable) are illustrated below.

a) Linear - positive   b) Linear - negative

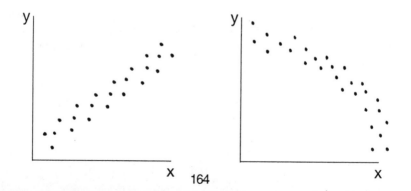

c) Curvilinear - positive

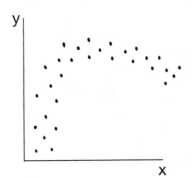

d) Curvilinear - negative

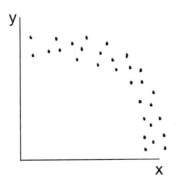

e) No relationship

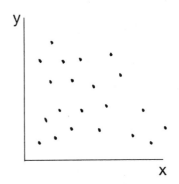

f) No relationship

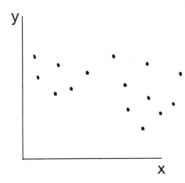

11.2 CORRELATION COEFFICIENT

The study of the strength of the relationship between X and Y is termed *correlation analysis,* and the *correlation coefficient* is calculated to measure the strength as well as the direction of this linear relationship. The correlation coefficient can range from -1.0 to +1.0, where -1.0 indicates a perfect negative or inverse relationship and +1.0 indicates a perfect positive or direct relationship. When either of these situations occur, all data points within the scatter diagram will fall directly on the regression line. A value of 0 for the correlation coefficient signifies no linear relationship between X and Y. As a general guideline, we can state that a value of .8 or above (either positive or negative) is an indication of a fairly strong relationship, while a value of .3 or less (either positive or negative) is an indication of a weak relationship between X and Y.

The correlation coefficient may be calculated using population data or sample data. The two differ only in certain symbolism.

Population Correlation Coefficient

$$\rho = \frac{N\Sigma XY - \Sigma X \Sigma Y}{\sqrt{\left[N\left(\Sigma X^2\right) - \left(\Sigma X\right)^2\right]\left[N\left(\Sigma Y^2\right) - \left(\Sigma Y\right)^2\right]}}$$

where: ρ (Greek letter rho) = symbol for population correlation coefficient.

Sample Correlation Coefficient

$$r = \frac{n\Sigma XY - \Sigma X \Sigma Y}{\sqrt{\left[n\left(\Sigma X^2\right) - \left(\Sigma X\right)^2\right]\left[n\left(\Sigma Y^2\right) - \left(\Sigma Y\right)^2\right]}}$$

where: r = symbol for sample correlation coefficient.

EXAMPLE:

In the previous chapter, we used an example in which we compared the percentage of defectives (Y) with the speed of the machine in rpm (X). Using this same data set, we can determine the correlation coefficient assuming that these data represent a sample of size 10 selected from a population.

SOLUTION:

Since we have already determined the regression equation and the standard error of the estimate, we have all the summations required to calculate the correlation coefficient:

$$n = 10 \qquad \Sigma X^2 = 45300$$
$$\Sigma XY = 1265 \qquad \Sigma Y^2 = 36.69$$
$$\Sigma X = 660$$
$$\Sigma Y = 18.3$$

Therefore,

$$r = \frac{10(1,265) - (660)(18.3)}{\sqrt{\left[10(45,300) - (660)^2\right]\left[10(36.69) - (18.3)^2\right]}}$$

$$= \frac{12,650 - 12,078}{\sqrt{(453,000 - 435,600)(366.9 - 334.89)}}$$

$$= \frac{572}{\sqrt{(17,400)(32.01)}}$$

$$= \frac{572}{\sqrt{556,974}}$$

$$= 572 / 746.307 = .766.$$

Since $r = .766$, which is almost .8, this indicates that the relationship between percentage of defectives and speed of machine is fairly strong and is positive.

11.3 COEFFICIENT OF DETERMINATION

The *coefficient of determination* is the correlation coefficient squared and *tells us the percentage of the variation in the dependent variable (Y) which is explained by the variation in the independent variable (X)*. It may range from 0.0% to 100.0%.

The coefficient of determination is simply denoted as follows:

ρ^2 for the population

r^2 for the sample.

EXAMPLE:

In our previous example comparing speed of machine (X) with percentage of defectives *(Y)*, we calculated the correlation coefficient to be .766. What is the coefficient of determination?

SOLUTION:

The coefficient of determination is:

$$r^2 = (.766)^2 = .5868$$
$$\text{or } 58.68\%.$$

This tells us that 58.68% of the variation in the percentage of defectives is explained by the variation in the speed of the machine. This means that the remainder of the variation, 41.32% (100% - 58.68%), is attributable to other factors. We can speculate that these other factors might include machine operators, materials used, etc.

11.4   HYPOTHESIS TESTING

Just as we are able to test for a significant β (slope of the regression equation), we may also test for a significant ρ (correlation coefficient in the population). We may follow our same five step outline for hypothesis testing, making the appropriate symbolic changes.

EXAMPLE:

Test at the .05 level of significance to determine if the correlation coefficient is significantly different from 0 when comparing speed of machine with percentage of defectives.

SOLUTION:

1. $H_0: \rho = 0$
    $H_1: \rho \neq 0$ (2-tailed test)

This hypothesis setup is for testing only for a significant difference with no directional difference implied. If a directional difference is important, we may test for this as well by using either < or > for the alternative hypothesis.

2. $n = 10$
    $r = .766$
    $\alpha = .05$

3. The Student's t-distribution with n-2 degrees of freedom is appropriate for this test.

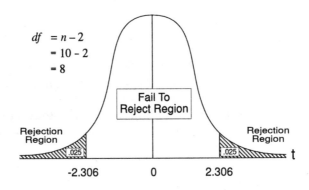

$$df = n - 2$$
$$= 10 - 2$$
$$= 8$$

Therefore, $t = \pm2.306$.

4.

$$t = \frac{r}{\sqrt{\dfrac{1 - r^2}{n - 2}}}$$

$$= \frac{.766}{\sqrt{\dfrac{1 - .766^2}{10 - 2}}}$$

$$= \frac{.766}{\sqrt{\dfrac{1 - .5868}{8}}}$$

$$= \frac{.766}{\sqrt{.05166}}$$

$$= \frac{.766}{.22728}$$

$$= 3.37$$

5. Since $3.37 > \pm 2.306$, we should reject H_0: and accept H_1:. This test concludes that ρ is significantly different from 0 in the population, i.e., there is a significant relationship between X and Y in the population. However, there is a 5% chance that we have reached an incorrect conclusion, i.e., committed a Type I error.

CHAPTER 12

MULTIPLE REGRESSION ANALYSIS

12.1 MULTIPLE REGRESSION MODEL

In Chapter 3, we introduced simple linear regression, a model depicting the linear relationship between one dependent variable (Y) and one independent variable (X). The multiple regression model is an extension of this model in which more than one independent variable is included. Again, we will deal only with the linear (straight line) relationship between the dependent variable and independent variables; curvilinear relationships are beyond the scope of our discussion.

The multiple regression model is:

$$Y_i = \alpha + \beta_1 X_{i1} + \beta_2 X_{i2} + \beta_3 X_{i3} + ...\beta_k X_{ik} + \varepsilon_i$$

where: Y_i = value of the dependent variable,

α = intercept, or the value of Y when all Xs are 0,

β_j = the coefficients of the X_{ij}s or the change in Y_i per unit change in X_j,

ε_i = the random error term,

X_{ij}s = values of the independent variables.

The assumptions of the model are very similar to those of the simple linear model; i.e.,

1. Y_i is a random variable, normally distributed at each value of X_{ij}.

171

2. X_{ij}s are non-random, predetermined values which are independent of each other,

3. ε_i is NID $(0, \sigma)$.

These assumptions must be met when either estimation or hypothesis testing is applied while using multiple regression analysis. It is not necessary that they be met, however, if we are not inferring our results beyond the data set being analyzed.

12.2 MULTIPLE REGRESSION EQUATION

The multiple regression equation will be illustrated by using the simplest form; i.e., two independent variables. As this example will illustrate, the computations for even a model including two independent variables are very cumbersome. Beyond this, it is not practical to attempt to solve a multiple regression problem without the use of the computer.

The regression equation for two independent variables is presented below:

$$Y_i = a + b_1 X_{i1} + b_2 X_{i2}$$

where: Y_i = values of the dependent variable,

X_{i1} = values of the first independent variable,

X_{i2} = values of the second independent variable.

and:

$$b_1 = \frac{\left(\Sigma X_1 Y - n\overline{X}_1\overline{Y}\right)\left(\Sigma X_2^2 - n\overline{X}_2^2\right) - \left(\Sigma X_2 Y - n\overline{X}_2\overline{Y}\right)\left(\Sigma X_1 X_2 - n\overline{X}_1\overline{X}_2\right)}{\left(\Sigma X_1^2 - n\overline{X}_1^2\right)\left(\Sigma X_2^2 - n\overline{X}_2^2\right) - \left(\Sigma X_1 X_2 - n\overline{X}_1\overline{X}_2\right)^2}$$

$$b_2 = \frac{\left(\Sigma X_2 Y - n\overline{X}_2\overline{Y}\right)\left(\Sigma X_1^2 - nX_1^2\right) - \left(\Sigma X_1 Y - n\overline{X}_1\overline{Y}\right)\left(\Sigma X_1 X_2 - n\overline{X}_1\overline{X}_2\right)}{\left(\Sigma X_1^2 - n\overline{X}_1^2\right)\left(\Sigma X_2^2\right) - \left(\Sigma X_1 X_2 - n\overline{X}_1\overline{X}_2\right)^2}$$

$$a = \overline{Y} - b_1\overline{X}_1 - b_2\overline{X}_2$$

EXAMPLE:

A group of 10 investors was selected and their long-term net gain or loss was compared with their age and their annual income. The following data resulted:

Y = Net Gain (Loss) (1,000s)	X_1 = Age	X_2 = Annual Income (1,000s)
-429	46	100
6	30	40
0	41	63
-63	50	60
-44	56	80
-8	47	35
-19	49	110
-26	74	28
-32	76	100
-5	41	32

Compute the regression equation.

SOLUTION:

We will need the following summations for our calculation.

$$\Sigma X_2 Y \qquad \Sigma X_2$$
$$\Sigma X_1 Y \qquad \Sigma X_1^2$$
$$\Sigma X_1 X_2 \qquad \Sigma X_2^2$$
$$\Sigma X_1 \qquad \Sigma Y$$
$$n$$

Therefore, a table will be constructed to include the necessary columns for these summations.

Y	X_1	X_2	$X_1 X_2$	$X_1 Y$	$X_2 Y$	X_1^2	ΣX_2^2
-429	46	100	4,600	-19,734	-42,900	2,116	10,000
6	30	40	1,200	180	240	900	1,600
0	41	63	2,583	0	0	1,681	3,969
-63	50	60	3,000	-3,150	-3,780	2,500	3,600
-44	56	80	4,480	-2,464	-3,520	3,136	6,400
-8	47	35	1,645	-376	-280	2,209	1,225
-19	49	110	5,390	-931	-2,090	2,401	12,100
-26	74	28	2,072	-1,924	-728	5,476	784
-32	76	100	7,600	-2,432	-3,200	5,776	10,000
-5	41	32	1,312	-205	-160	1,681	1,024
TOTAL 620	510	648	33,882	-31,036	-56,418	27,876	50,702

$$\overline{X}_1 = \frac{510}{10} = 51 \qquad \overline{X}_2 = \frac{648}{10} = 64.8 \qquad \overline{Y} = \frac{-620}{10} = -62$$

$$b_1 = \frac{\left[-56418 - 10(64.8)(-62)\right]\left[33882 - 10(51)(64.8)\right]}{\left[27876 - 10(51)^2\right]\left[50702 - 10(64.8)^2\right] - \left[33882 - 10(51)(64.8)\right]^2}$$

$$= \frac{(-31036 + 31620)(50702 - 41990.4) - (56418 + 40176)(33882 - 33048)}{(27876 - 26010)(50702 - 41990.4) - (33882 - 33048)^2}$$

$$= M\frac{(584)(8711.6) - (-16242)(834)}{(1866)(8711.6) - (834)^2}$$

$$= \frac{5,087,574.4 + 13,545,828}{16,255,845.6 - 695,556}$$

$$= 1.1975$$

$$b_2 = \frac{\left[-56418 - 10(64.8)(-62)\right]\left[27876 - 10(51^2)\right] - \left[-31036 - 10(51)(-62)\right]\left[33882 - 10(51)(64.8)\right]}{\left[27876 - 10(51)^2\right]\left[50702 - 10(64.8)^2\right] - \left[33882 - 10(51)(64.8)\right]^2}$$

$$= \frac{(-16242)(1866) - (584)(834)}{15,560,289.6}$$

$$= \frac{-30,307,572 - 487,056}{15,560,289.6}$$

$$= -1.9791$$

$$a = -62 - (1.1975)(51) - (01.9791)(64.8)$$

$$= -62 - 61.0725 + 128.24568$$

$$= 5.1731$$

Therefore:
$$Y = 5.1731 + 1.1975X_1 - 1.9791X_2,$$
which says that as X_1 (Age) increases by 1 year, Y (Net Gain) increases by 1.1975 or \$1,197.50. Similarly, as X_2 (Annual Income) increases by \$1,000, Net Gain (Loss) decreases by 1.9791 or \$1,979.10.

12.3 INFERENCE TECHNIQUES

In simple linear regression analysis, we illustrated the concept of testing for a significant β in the population. We may apply the same theory here and extend it to cover the model in general as well as each of the β_is included in the particular model. For example, if we have a multiple regression model which includes four independent variables, we first test to determine if, collectively, the model is significant. That is, we test the null hypothesis (H_0: all β's $= 0$) against the alternative hypothesis (H_1: at least one $\beta_i \neq 0$). We perform this overall test using the F-distribution which we introduced in discussing ANOVA in Chapter 2. Once this test is performed, if we reject the null hypothesis in favor of the alternative and conclude that at least one $\beta_i \neq 0$, we may then test each β_i in the model individually. These individual tests are typically performed using either the Student's t-distribution, just as we illustrated in testing β in the simple linear model, or the F-test. Those variables with a significant β should remain in the model while those testing not significant should be removed from the model, with revised estimators being calculated. We will illustrate this concept with a computer example due to the mathematical cumbersomeness when attempting to work with more than two independent variables.

12.4 COMPUTER OUTPUT

EXAMPLE:
The Zinc Corp. is interested in the relationship between sales of their products, advertising expenditures, number of salesmen, and research and development budget. They randomly select 30 products which they manufacture and collect the data shown below.

Products	Annual Sales (\$1,000s)	Annual Advertising Expenditure (\$100s)	Number of Salesmen	Annual R&D Expenditure (\$100s)
1	88.3	50.2	6	12.8
2	89.5	81.9	6	8.1
3	76.7	64.4	3	9.5
4	88.7	71.6	3	10.4

Products	Annual Sales ($1,000s)	Annual Advertising Expenditure ($100s)	Number of Salesmen	Annual R&D Expenditure ($100s)
5	55.7	44.2	2	5.2
6	48.4	34.0	1	5.0
7	38.4	37.2	4	10.7
8	93.5	63.1	5	10.6
9	92.1	79.6	3	9.5
10	71.3	69.0	1	6.0
11	65.3	44.6	3	6.7
12	94.5	102.2	3	12.2
13	54.9	52.2	1	5.4
14	109.6	91.7	7	15.5
15	97.1	69.6	4	9.0
16	65.7	54.9	8	9.2
17	78.6	68.3	4	7.7
18	63.2	56.8	6	10.1
19	86.5	63.4	1	10.1
20	70.7	54.2	1	4.9
21	83.3	68.1	6	7.2
22	65.4	44.6	3	7.4
23	89.1	59.9	3	11.5
24	84.2	72.7	5	9.1
25	79.4	65.2	4	9.0
26	99.8	64.7	5	12.1
27	63.6	51.1	3	4.5
28	73.2	44.9	1	6.4
29	64.7	59.8	2	7.5
30	86.6	76.7	5	7.9

Compute a multiple regression model in which the dependent variable *(Y)* is sales and the independent variables are advertising expenditure, number of salesmen, and research and development expenditure.

SOLUTION:

The SPSS (Statistical Package for the Social Sciences) solution is as follows:

```
                  MULTIPLE REGRESSION MODEL EXAMPLE
FILE                    NONAME (CREATION DATE = JULY 25, 1990)

                   MULTIPLE REGRESSION     VARIABLE LIST 1
                                           REGRESSION LIST 1

DEPENDENT VARIABLE..              SALES
VARIABLE(S) ENTERED ON STEP NUMBER 1..       R&D
                                         ADV
                                         NUMBER
```

176

```
MULTIPLE R   0.83459    ANALYSIS OF VARIANCE DF   SUM OF SQUARES   MEAN SQUARE    F
R SQUARE     0.69654    REGRESSION           3.     5501.00336    1833.66779  19.89256
ADJUSTED
R SQUARE     0.66152    RESIDUAL            26.     2396.64293      92.17857
STANDARD
ERROR        9.60097
```

VARIABLES IN THE EQUATION

VARIABLE	B	BETA	STD. ERROR B	F
R&D	2.032272	0.32651	0.88958	5.219
ADV	.6630343	0.62226	0.13331	24.736
NUMBER	-.9677280D-02	-0.00115	1.10522	0.000
(CONSTANT)	18.48613			

* ALL VARIABLES ARE IN THE EQUATION.
STATISTICS WHICH CANNOT BE COMPUTED ARE PRINTED AS ALL
NINES.

VARIABLES NOT IN THE EQUATION

VARIABLE	BETA IN	PARTIAL	TOLERANCE	F

The interpretation of this output may be analyzed in the following steps:

1. Test the null hypothesis.

$$H_0: \text{all } \beta_i = 0$$

$$H_1: \text{at least one } \beta_i \neq 0$$

This is the overall F-test, and the value used to test this hypothesis is the F-value from the analysis of variance section of the printout ($F = 19.893$). This value is tested just as we did before by using the regression degrees of freedom υ_1 (numerator) and the residual degrees of freedom υ_2 (denominator). These degrees of freedom determine an F-value from the table for some specified level of significance ($\alpha = .05$).

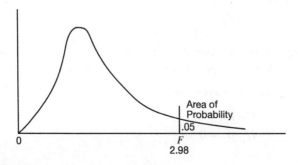

Therefore, $F = 2.98$.

Since $19.893 > 2.98$, we reject H_0: and accept H_1: which concludes that at least one variable in the model is significant. We certainly hope that this is the case; otherwise we have totally worthless data and must identify new variables for the analysis.

2. Now that we have concluded that at least one of the independent variables is significant, we must test each one individually to determine which are significant and which, if any, are not. The bottom left section of the printout, headed "Variables in the equation," is used for these tests. The F-values in the far right hand column are used. Each of these values will be tested against an F-table value where the numerator degrees of freedom is 1, and the denominator degrees of freedom is 26 (the same as it was for the overall F-test). This table value is:

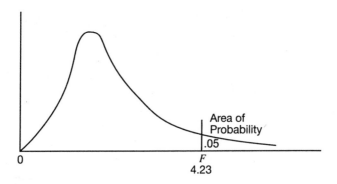

Therefore, $F = 4.23$.

Therefore, we test the following null hypotheses.

1. **For R&D**

$$H_0: \beta_1 = 0$$
$$H_1: \beta_1 \neq 0$$

Since $F = 5.219$ is > 4.23, we reject the null hypothesis in favor of the alternative and conclude that R&D expenditures is a significant variable in helping to explain sales variations.

2. **For Advertising**

$$H_0: \beta_2 = 0$$
$$H_1: \beta_2 \neq 0$$

178

Since $F = 24.736$ is > 4.23, we reject H_0: and accept H_1: and conclude that advertising is also significant in explaining sales variations, when R&D is also included in the model.

3. For Number

$$H_0: \beta_3 = 0$$
$$H_1: \beta_3 \neq 0$$

Since $F = 0.000$ is < 4.23, we cannot reject H_0:. Therefore, we conclude that the number of salesmen does not have any significant effect on the amount of sales.

3. Since the number of salesmen is not a significant variable in explaining sales, we now remove it from the model and run the analysis again without this variable. The result follows:

MULTIPLE REGRESSION MODEL EXAMPLE

FILE   NONAME (CREATION DATE = JULY 25, 1990)

MULTIPLE REGRESSION   VARIABLE LIST 1
REGRESSION LIST 1

DEPENDENT VARIABLE..   SALES
VARIABLE(S) ENTERED ON STEP NUMBER 1..   R&D
ADV

MULTIPLE R	0.83459	ANALYSIS OF VARIANCE	DF	SUM OF SQUARES	MEAN SQUARE	F
R SQUARE	0.69654	REGRESSION	2.	5500.9962	2750.498159	30.98636
ADJUSTED						
R SQUARE	0.67406	RESIDUAL	27.	2396.65000	88.76481	
STD. ERROR	9.42151					

VARIABLES IN THE EQUATION

VARIABLE	B	BETA	STD. ERROR B	F
R&D	2.028479	0.32590	0.76250	7.077
ADV	.6629567	0.62219	0.13053	25.795
(CONSTANT)	18.4888			

* ALL VARIABLES ARE IN THE EQUATION.

STATISTICS WHICH CANNOT BE COMPUTED ARE PRINTED AS ALL NINES.

VARIABLES NOT IN THE EQUATION

VARIABLE	BETA IN	PARTIAL	TOLERANCE	F

Now the model becomes:

$$Y = \alpha + \beta_1 X_1 + \beta_2 X_2 + \varepsilon_i$$

and the equation is:

$$Y = 18.489 + 2.028 \text{ R\&D} + .663 \text{ ADV}.$$

These coefficients indicate that:

1. For each additional $100 of R&D investment, sales increase by 2.028, or $2,028; and

2. Given that R&D is in the model, with each additional $100 spent on advertising, sales increase by .663, or $663.

The information below is also important for interpretation of the output.

1. **Multiple R**

   This is the multiple correlation coefficient and explains the collective strength of the independent variables as they are related to the dependent variable. The value of .83459 indicates that this relationship is strong.

2. **R-Square**

   This is the coefficient of determination (r^2) which we introduced in Chapter 3. The value of .69654 tells us that 69.654% of the variation in sales is attributed jointly to advertising dollars and R&D budget. This means that the remaining variation (100% - 69.654%) is attributable to factors which were not included in the model. Note that an adjusted R-square is also given. This is an adjustment for the number of independent variables included in the model.

3. **Standard Error**

   This is the standard error of the estimate $(S_{y \cdot x})$ which we introduced when discussing simple linear regression. It measures the average variation of the actual values of Y from the estimated values of Y predicted from the equation. We may use this value in making confidence interval estimates just as we did in the case of simple linear regression.

4. **Beta**

   The values of beta are the coefficients (β_is) standardized so that they may be compared against each other even though their original measurements may be in different units. The larger the value of beta, the greater is the contribution of the variable to the model. In this case, advertising, with a beta of .622, has a stronger relationship with sales than does R&D, with a beta of .325.

5. **Standard Error of _B_**

These are the standard error values for each of the β_is (coefficients). They are equivalent to $S_{y \cdot x}$ which we discussed in simple linear regression, and are used in arriving at the F-value for the test of each individual variable.

In this example, initially all three independent variables were entered simultaneously into the model. The insignificant variable was then eliminated from the model, resulting in the reduced model containing two independent variables, which we analyzed.

Other variable selection techniques exist. The *forward selection* procedure allows for entering the variables one at a time, beginning with the one which has the strongest ability to explain the variation in the dependent variable and continuing on until all variables have been considered. The *backward elimination* procedure is the reverse of forward selection in that all variables are in the model originally and independent variables which have the least explanatory power are removed from the model, with the procedure continuing on until all variables have been considered. Regardless of which procedure is used, we should eventually end up with a model which is significant overall and in which all independent variables are significant.

12.5 DUMMY VARIABLES

In the two previous examples, the dependent variables as well as all independent variables were quantitative or numerical. That is, they were quantitative in the sense that, by nature, they had a real or true numerical meaning. Many times, however, there is a need in regression models to include qualitative or verbal independent variables. Examples of this type might be sex, marital status, or educational level. When a variable such as one of these is included in a regression model, it must be assigned a numerical value. For example, if we included sex, we might let 0 stand for male and 1 stand for female. Once we assign a numerical value to a qualitative variable, it is referred to as a **dummy variable**.

The proper way to assign codes to dummy variables is outlined below.

1. When a qualitative variable (e.g., $X_1 = $ sex) has only two possible options, we use the following format for including the dummy variable in a regression model:

SEX: X_1 = 0 for males
       X_1 = 1 for females.

Now, let's assume that we have a regression equation which includes a second independent variable (X_2) which is income, and that our dependent variable is sales of some product. Assume the following equation resulted when analyzing the data:

$$Y = 10.67 + 1.072X_1 - 6.73X_2.$$

The coefficient of X_1 indicates that sales of the product would be predicted to be 1.072 units higher for females than for males. This is due to the fact that if we substitute X_1 = 0 (for male), no change in $\hat{Y}$ would occur. However, if we substitute X_1 = 1 (for females), the value of $\hat{Y}$ will increase by 1.072 units. This estimate, of course, would take into account the value of X_2 (income) simultaneously with sex.

2. When a qualitative variable has more than two possible options or categories, we must create a number of dummy variables equal to the number of options less 1. For example, if marital status is to be included in the model and there are three options (single, married, and widowed or divorced) we must create two dummy variables. The proper way to do this is as follows:

Single: X_1 = 1 if single
        X_1 = 0 if otherwise
Married: X_2 = 1 if married
         X_2 = 0 if otherwise.

If X_1 = 0 and X_2 = 0, this implies that the individual is divorced or widowed. Since this is the case, there is no need for identifying a third variable for "divorced or widowed." Suppose we calculate the following regression equation where we are predicting grocery sales *(Y)* using the independent variables of income (X_3) and marital status $(X_1$ and $X_2)$:

$$Y = 240.6 - 16.2X_1 + 10.4X_2 + 1.75X_3.$$

This equation predicts that the single person's ($X_1 = 1$) effect on grocery sales is -16.2 dollars when taking into account income (X_3) as well, while a married person's ($X_2 = 1$) effect is a positive 10.4 dollars when taking into account income (X_3) as well. The effect of the divorced or widowed person ($X_1 = X_2 = 0$) on grocery sales is 0, in the sense that this category serves as a "base" against which single and married people are compared. In comparing the three categories, if:

$X_1 = 1$ and $X_2 = 0$; $\hat{Y} = 240.6 - 16.2(1) + 10.4(0) + 1.75\,X_3$
$\qquad\qquad\qquad\quad \hat{Y} = 224.4 + 175\,X_3$

$X_2 = 0$ and $X_2 = 1$; $Y = 240.6 - 16.2(0) + 10.4(1) + 1.75\,X_3$
$\qquad\qquad\qquad\quad \hat{Y} = 251 + 1.75\,X_3$

$X_1 = 0$ and $X_2 = 0$; $\hat{Y} = 240.6 - 16.2(0) + 10.4(0) + 1.75\,X_3$
$\qquad\qquad\qquad\quad \hat{Y} = 240.6 + 1.75\,X_3$.

These comparisons illustrate that a person who is married purchases an average of $26.60 ($251 - $224.40) more than the single person and $10.40 ($251 - $240.60) more than the widowed/divorced individual.

Sometimes we see qualitative or categorical variables, such as those above, included in a regression model as a single variable and coded: 1 = single, 2 = married, and 3 = widowed or divorced. If this is the case, an implied assumption is that a constant difference exists between the categories, which typically cannot be defended. Thus, this should not be done. Using the procedure outlined above, however, allows for determining which option of the categorical variable has the most influence on the dependent variable (Y).

CHAPTER 13

NONPARAMETRIC TESTS

13.1 LEVELS OF MEASUREMENT

Measurement is defined as the assigning of numerical values to objects to represent quantities or attributes. Many times, the way that numbers are assigned, or the particular numbers themselves, may imply properties which do not truly exist in the data. Therefore, it is important that an understanding of measurement levels exists so that statistical methodology may be appropriately applied to the data at hand. There are four levels or scales which will be discussed.

a) **Nominal Scale**

Nominal scales are comprised of numbers used primarily for the purpose of identifying or categorizing individuals, objects, or events. An example is one which we have used earlier when we assigned the value of 0 to males and 1 to females when coding the variable sex for a multiple regression model. It should be noted that the code can be reversed as long as the proper identification is made and that the number "1" does not imply a superior position to the number "0." When assigning these codes, we must, however, be careful to code all members of a particular group in the same manner and we must also be sure that no two groups are assigned the same coded value.

b) **Ordinal Scale**

Ordinal scales are used primarily to rank items. They allow not only for indicating which objects have the same characteristic, but they also allow for specifying whether one object has more or less of the characteristic than does another object in the data set. However, the ordinal scale does not provide information on how much more or less of the characteristic one item possesses over another. Any values may be assigned to reflect this ranking since the difference in values is meaningless. For example, if we are using a scale of excellent, good, fair, or poor, we may assign:

1 = Poor		10 = Poor
2 = Fair		30 = Fair
3 = Good	or	40 = Good
4 = Excellent		50 = Excellent.

Whether or not it is possible to use an ordinal scale to assign numerals to objects depends on the attribute being ranked. That is, the attribute itself must possess the ordinal property if it is to be assigned meaningful ranks.

c) Interval Scale

Interval scales are used to rank items when equal distances on the scale may be assumed to represent equal differences in the property being measured and both the zero point and the unit of measurement are arbitrary. An example which might illustrate these properties is the variable temperature where the freezing point of water is 0 on the Centigrade scale and 32 on the Fahrenheit scale and either scale may be converted to the other through a mathematical relationship. Another example is an index number which requires an arbitrary zero point and equal intervals between scale values.

d) Ratio Scale

In addition to all the properties of interval scaled data, ratio scales have an absolute zero point which represents absence of the characteristic; therefore, it is legitimate to compare the absolute magnitude of the numbers. Examples are sales, market share, units produced, and advertising expenditures.

The level of the measurement scale dictates the statistical methodology which may be applied to a set of data. The more advanced scales, therefore, allow for more advanced statistical techniques. If data are interval scaled or ratio scaled and the underlying assumptions of the technique are met, virtually any statistical methodology may be applied. However, if data are either ordinal or nominal scaled, they do not possess the properties required for the more sophisticated techniques. Therefore, the most appropriate techniques for ordinal and nominal data are found in the branch of statistical methodology known as nonparametric statistics.

These techniques are "distribution free," in that they make no assumptions about the shape or condition of the underlying distributions from which data are collected. The procedures discussed in this chapter may be applied to either nominal or interval scaled data.

13.2 CHI-SQUARE GOODNESS-OF-FIT TESTS

The chi-square (x^2) distribution is yet one more distribution used in testing hypotheses. A chi-square table exists for reading critical values similar to those which we have studied for the Z-distribution, the t-distribution, and the F-distribution. The chi-square distribution is defined by the number of degrees of freedom and it changes shapes depending on the number of degrees of freedom (υ) for the particular problem. A very small value of υ will result in a distribution like the one sketched below.

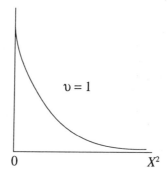

$\upsilon = 1$

0 \qquad\qquad X^2

Note that chi-square values range from 0 to infinity. As the number of degrees of freedom increases, the distribution takes on a shape much like the F-distribution and less skewness results as the value of υ becomes larger and larger.

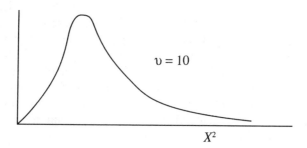

$\upsilon = 10$

X^2

The value of chi-square (X^2) is calculated from the following formula:

$$X^2 = \sum_{i=1}^{k} \left[\frac{(O_i - E_i)^2}{E_i} \right]$$

where: x^2 = chi-square,

O_i = the observed number of observations in each category (i),

E_i = the expected number of observations in each category (i) given that the null hypothesis is true,

k = number of categories being investigated.

A goodness-of-fit test is one in which we test the null hypothesis that some particular data of interest take on a particular shape in the population. The shape tested might be, for example, the normal distribution, the binomial distribution, the Poisson distribution, the uniform distribution, or any other "arbitrary distribution" which might be pertinent for the particular situation at hand. Examples illustrating the uniform distribution and an "arbitrary distribution" will be presented. Examples illustrating normal, Poisson, and binomial distributions may be found in more detailed statistical textbooks.

EXAMPLE 1:

A mail-order house receives an average of 700 orders per week (7 days). The assumption of the sales manager is that orders are fairly evenly distributed among days of the week. In order to test this assumption, he randomly selects a number of weeks and calculates the average number of orders placed on each day of the week. The results are shown below.

Average Number of Orders

Sundays	80
Mondays	150
Tuesdays	105
Wednesdays	75
Thursdays	85
Fridays	95
Saturdays	110
	700

Test at the .05 level of significance to determine if the sales manager's assumption is substantiated.

SOLUTION:

1. H_0: The number of orders in the population follows a *uniform* distribution.

   H_1: The number of orders in the population does not follow a *uniform* distribution.

2. $k = 7$

   $N = 700$

   $\alpha = .05$

   O_is are the values observed from the sample as presented.

3. The chi-square distribution is the appropriate one to use. The number of degrees of freedom is:

$$df = k\text{-}1 = 7\text{-}1 = 6,$$

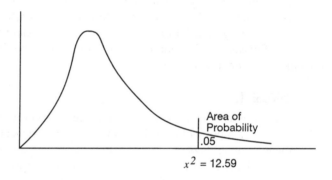

$$x^2 = 12.59$$

Therefore, $x^2 = 12.59$.

A goodness-of-fit test is always tested as a one-tailed test, with the value of α placed in the right tail, as illustrated above.

4. The values of E_i must be determined based on the assumption in the null hypothesis and the data collected for the sample. If we assume that orders are distributed uniformly, this implies that each day should have the same number of orders. In this case, that number is 100 orders (700/7 days = 100 per day). The most efficient means of calculating the value of x^2 is to set up a table reflecting the calculations.

O_i	E_i	$(O_i - E_i)$	$(O_i - E_i)^2$	$(O_i - E_i)^2/E_i$
80	100	-20	400	4.0
150	100	50	2500	25.0
105	100	5	25	.25
75	100	-25	625	6.25
85	100	-15	225	2.25
95	100	-5	25	.25
110	100	10	100	1.00
700	700	0		39.00

$$x^2 = \sum_{i=1}^{k}\left[\frac{(O_1 - E_i)^2}{E_i}\right]$$

$$= 39.00$$

5. Since 39.00 > 12.59, we reject the null hypothesis (H_0:) and accept the alternative hypothesis (H_1:). This concludes that the orders are not distributed uniformly among days of the week. However, remember, as in all hypothesis testing results, when we reject the H_0:, we must consider the possibility that we have arrived at an erroneous conclusion; i.e., we have a 5% chance of our conclusion being in error. This conclusion, however, should have implications for management relative to the scheduling of workers to handle the orders.

EXAMPLE 2:

The Video Spot rents movies and games. The manager of the Spot contends that his rentals are very heavily weighted toward Fridays and Saturdays. He believes that these two days make up 60% of his total business, while Sundays make up approximately 25%, and Mondays through Thursdays, the remaining 15%. He randomly samples rentals over the past 5 years and collects the following rental data information.

Days	Average Number of Rentals
Friday and Saturday	160
Sunday	70
Monday - Thursday	20
	250

Test at the .01 level of significance to determine if the manager's contention can be substantiated.

SOLUTION:

1. H_0: Rentals follow the pattern as indicated by the store's manager.

    H_1: Rentals do not follow this pattern.

2. $K = 3$
    $N = 250$
    $\alpha = 01$
    O_is are as specified above.

3. The chi-square distribution is appropriate here, and

    $$df = k{-}1 = 3{-}1 = 2$$

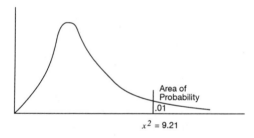

Therefore, $x^2 = 9.21$.

4. The values of E_i must be determined based on the specified distribution in the problem. That is, the manager assumes the distribution of movie rentals to be 60% on Fridays and Saturdays, 25% on Sundays, and 15% for the remaining 4 days. Therefore, we must determine the number of rentals expected for each of these by multiplying each percentage by the total of 250 rentals. For example, the first E_i is 250 (.6) = 150.

5. Since 9.734 > 9.21, we reject H_0: and accept H_1:. Therefore, we conclude that the rentals do not follow the pattern identified by the store manager. However, there is a 1% chance that we are in error with our conclusion.

13.3 TEST FOR INDEPENDENCE

The chi-square distribution is also useful if it is desired to test for statistical independence between two categorical (nominal scale) variables. Here the calculation is done just as we previously illustrated for the goodness-of-fit test in that observed values are compared with expected values in order to determine if the differences are extreme enough to reflect a true relationship. The same equation is used, but we will use a double subscript to reflect the summation over both rows and columns of the contingency table.

$$x^{2^*} = \sum_{i=1}^{k} \sum_{j=1}^{1} \frac{\left(O_{ij} - E_{ij} \right)^2}{E_{ij}}$$

Tests of independence are set up in a ***contingency table*** format which provides the number of observations that have the joint characteristics of the two variables of interest. An example can best illustrate.

EXAMPLE:

Suppose data were collected for comparing sex against color preference in automobiles. Males and females were questioned as to their preference among three colors: white, red, and black. The data were set up in a contingency table where there are two rows (male, female) and three columns (white, red, black), i.e., a 2 x 3 contingency table.

AUTOMOBILE
Color Preference

	White	Red	Black	TOTAL
Male	30	160	80	270
Female	70	140	20	230
Total	100	300	100	500

Test at the .05 level in order to determine if sex and automobile color preference are independent.

SOLUTION:

1. H_0: Sex and automobile color preference are independent

H_1: Sex and automobile color preference are not independent

Another way of expressing these hypotheses:

H_0: There is no relationship between sex and automobile color preference

H_1: There is a relationship between sex and automobile color preference

2. $n = 500$
   $\alpha = .05$

3. The chi-square distribution is appropriate with:

$$df = (r-1)(c-1) \quad = \quad (2-1)(3-1)$$
$$= \quad 1 \times 2$$
$$= \quad 2$$

where: r = number of rows in contingency table

c = number of columns in contingency table.

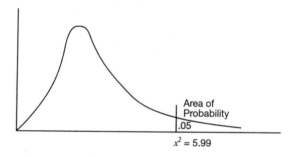

Therefore, $x^2 = 5.99$.

4. The E_{ij}s are again determined assuming that the null hypothesis is true and that there is no relationship between the two variables being studied. These values are determined using the following relationship:

192

$$E_{ij} = \frac{\sum\limits_{i=1}^{k} O_{ij}}{N} \times \sum\limits_{j=1}^{i})_{ij}$$

Therefore:

$$E_{11} = \frac{(O_{11} + O_{21})}{N} \times (O_{11} + O_{12} + O_{13})$$

$$= \frac{30 + 70}{500} \times (30 + 160 + 80)$$

$$= \frac{100}{500} \times 270$$

$$= 54$$

$$E_{12} = \frac{(O_{12} + O_{22})}{N} \times (O_{11} + O_{12} + O_{13})$$

$$= \frac{160 + 140}{500} \times 270$$

$$= \frac{300}{500} \times 270$$

$$= 54$$

$$E_{21} = \frac{(O_{21} + O_{22} + O_{23})}{N} \times (O_{11} + O_{21})$$

$$= \frac{230}{500} \times 100$$

$$= 46$$

$$E_{22} = \frac{230}{500} \times 300$$

$$= 138$$

$$E_{23} = \frac{230}{500} \times 100$$

$$= 46$$

We may now illustrate the contingency table showing both O_{ij}s and E_{ij}s.

AUTOMOBILE COLOR PREFERENCE
$$O_{ij}, E_{ij}$$

	White	Red	Black	TOTAL
Male	30, 54	160, 162	80, 54	270
Female	70, 46	140, 138	20, 46	230
Total	100	300	100	500

To calculate x^2, we set up the same table for calculation as before.

O_i	E_i	$(O_i - E_i)$	$(O_i - E_i)^2$	$(O_i - E_i)^2/E_i$
30	54	-24	576	10.667
70	46	24	576	12.522
160	162	-2	4	.025
140	138	2	4	.029
80	54	26	676	12.519
20	46	-26	676	14.696
500	500	0		50.458

$$x^2 = \sum \left[\frac{(O - E^2)}{E} \right]$$

$$= 50.458$$

5. Since $50.458 > 5.99$, we reject H_0: and accept H_1:. This concludes that sex and color preference are not independent or that these two variables are related. These results, together with the 30, 54, 70, 46, O_{ij}, and E_{ij} figures in the cells of the table, indicate that females tend to have a greater preference for white cars. Similarly, males tend to prefer black cars, and red cars are preferred almost equally by the two sexes. Again, as with all hypothesis testing problems, if we reject H_0: there is a chance of error in our conclusion. In this case, the probability of this error is 5%, the level of significance.

Contingency tables may contain as many rows and columns as is necessary for the problem at hand. However, there is a requirement in working with the chi-square distribution for both tests of independence and good-ness-of-fit tests that all E_is be ≥ 5. The reason for this is that small values of E_i tend to inflate the value of x^2 and might affect it enough to conclude that the null hypothesis should be rejected, when actually it should not be rejected. When any E_i is < 5, adjacent categories should be combined until all E_is are ≥ 5.

13.4   SPEARMAN'S RANK CORRELATION

In chapter 4, we introduced the correlation coefficient (ρ or r), which is a measure of the strength of the linear relationship between two variables. Spearman's rank correlation is also a measure of the strength of the relationship between two variables, but it only requires that the data be ordinal scaled, whereas the calculation of ρ or r requires the data to be at interval or ratio scaled.

The formula for calculation of Spearman's rank correlation coefficient is:

$$r_s = 1 - \frac{6 \sum_{i=1}^{n} D_i^2}{n(n^2 - 1)}$$

where: r_s = notation for Spearman's rank correlation,

D_i = the difference in the ranks of the ith pair of observations,

n = number of pairs of observations.

EXAMPLE:

The sales manager of the Wood Grocery Company believes that there is a relationship between sales volume of the individual salesman and personality traits. He therefore determines a personality score for each salesman and ranks them according to the score. He also determines total annual sales volume ($) for each salesman. The results are following.

Y = Sales ($)	X = Rank of Personality Score
1,000,000	1 = highest
3,500,000	2
3,000,000	3
5,000,000	4
800,000	5
1,250,000	6

Y = Sales (\$)	X = Rank of Personality Score
750,000	7
1,000,000	8
99,000	9
900,000	10 = lowest

Calculate the Spearman's rank correlation coefficient.

SOLUTION:

We first must rank the sales so that both variables are in the same form.

Y_i = Rank of Sales	Y_i = Rank of Personality Score	D_i	D_i^2
5.5	1	4.5	20.25
2	2	0	0
3	3	0	0
1	4	-3	9
8	5	3	9
4	6	-2	4
9	7	2	4
4.5	8	3.5	12.25
10	9	1	1
7	10	-3	9
			68.5

$$r_s = 1 - \frac{6\sum_{i=1}^{n} D_i^2}{n(n^2 - 1)}$$

$$= 1 - \frac{6(68.5)}{10(10^2 - 1)}$$

$$= 1 - \frac{411}{10(99)}$$

197

$$= 1 - \frac{411}{990}$$

$$= 1 - 0.415$$

$$= .585$$

This Spearman's rank correlation coefficient can be interpreted in the same way as the correlation coefficient that was discussed in Chapter 4. The value r_s = .585 indicates a moderate, but not strong (r_s < .8), correlation. Note that two salesmen had sales of $1,000,000, resulting in a tie for fifth place. When this occurs, we account for this by assigning the average rank that all tied positions would take to all observations involved. In this case, since two values were tied for fifth place, the rank assigned was the average of the fifth and sixth place or [(5 + 6)/2 = 5.5]. If, for example, three values were tied for sixth place, all 3 would be assigned the rank of 7; i.e., [(6 + 7 + 8)/3 = 7].

Also note in this example that sales is ratio scaled while personality score is ordinal. Therefore, we were forced to reduce ratio data to ordinal data so that this Spearman's rank procedure could be applied. This illustrates an example where our two variables being studied are different in level of measurement. Many times this is the case; however, it is not uncommon for both variables to be ordinal.

Just as we were able to test for a significant correlation in Chapter 4, we may test for a significant correlation when applying the Spearman's rank procedure. As long as we have at least 10 pairs of observations, the procedure is exactly the same as that previously illustrated in Chapter 4.

EXAMPLE:
Test at the .05 level of significance to determine if the correlation coefficient in the previous example is significant in the population.

SOLUTION:
1. H_0: Sales and personality are not related
   H_1: Sales and personality are related

2. n = 10
   α = .05
   r_s = .585

3. The Student's t-distribution is appropriate with:

$$df = n - 2$$
$$= 10 - 2 = 8$$
$$t_{(.05/2, df = 8)} = \pm 2.306$$

4.

$$t = \frac{r_2}{\sqrt{\dfrac{\left(1 - r_s^2\right)}{n - 2}}}$$

$$= \frac{0.585}{\sqrt{\dfrac{1 - (.585)^2}{8}}}$$

$$= \frac{.585}{\sqrt{\dfrac{0.658}{8}}}$$

$$= \frac{0.585}{.2867}$$

$$= 2.04$$

5. Since 2.04 < 2.306, we fail to reject H_0:, which indicates that the value of r_s is not sufficient to allow us to conclude a significant relationship between sales and personality.

13.5 MANN-WHITNEY U TEST

The Mann-Whitney U test is the counterpart to the two independent samples t-test. The U test may be applied as long as we have at least ordinal scaled data. It is generally applied when the data are in the form of ranks or if the assumption of normal populations, as required by the *t*-test, cannot be substantiated.

The procedure involves ranking the observations from the two samples combined together as one group and then summing the ranks for the individual groups. We then calculate a value of U for each group.

$$U_1 = n_1 n_2 + \frac{n_1(n_1 + 1)}{2} - R_1$$

$$U_2 = n_1 n_2 + \frac{n_2(n_2 + 1)}{2} - R_2$$

where: R_1 = Σ ranks of first sample,

R_2 = ranks of second sample.

One of these values of U will be the test statistic (U test) and will be used in the formula for calculation purposes. The rules to apply in order to determine which value should be used are as follows.

1. If we have a two-tailed test, either U_1 or U_2 may be used and the final result will be the same. However, if we are testing a one-tailed alternate hypothesis, we must select the value of U accordingly.

2. a) If the rejection region is in the left tail of the distribution, we will use the smaller value of U in our formula.
   b) If the rejection region is in the right tail of the distribution, we will use the larger value of U in our formula.

As long as n_1 and n_2 are 10 or larger, the distribution of U will be approximately normally distributed. The value of Z is calculated using

$$Z = \frac{U_{test} - \frac{n_1 n_2}{2}}{\sqrt{\frac{n_1 n_2 (n_1 n_2 + 1)}{12}}}$$

EXAMPLE:

Two comparably sized trucking companies, Transport and Carrier, both haul goods across country. It is desired to determine if there is a

200

significant difference in the average annual mileage figures of the two companies. The data are available in ratio scale; however, it is not reasonable to assume normal populations for miles traveled. Test at the .01 level to determine if a significant difference exists, using the data specified below.

Annual Miles Traveled (Millions) Transport	Annual Miles Traveled (Millions) Carrier
100	350
750	100
440	110
220	200
630	280
250	200
600	100
525	320
800	850
600	350
	100
	110

SOLUTION:

1. $H_0: \mu_1 = \mu_2$
   $H_1: \mu_1 \neq \mu_2$ (2-tailed test)

2. $n_1 = 10$
   $n_2 = 12$
   $\alpha = .01$

3. Since both n_1 and n_2 are ≥ 10, we may use the Z-distribution.

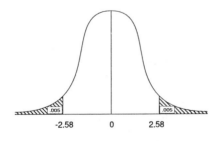

-2.58   0   2.58

Therefore, $Z = \pm 2.58$.

4. In order to calculate Z, we must rank the data from the two samples collectively. However, the process must allow for us to determine the sums of the ranks individually.

201

Therefore, the following table is set up.

Annual Miles Traveled (Millions) Transport	Rank	Annual Miles Traveled (Millions) Carrier	Rank
100	1	360	14
750	20	102	2
440	15	210	8
220	9	200	6
630	19	280	11
250	10	205	7
600	17	105	3
525	16	320	12
800	21	850	22
610	18	350	13
	$R_1 = 146$	109	4
		110	5
			$R_2 = 107$

$$U_1 = 10(12) + \frac{10(10+1)}{2} - 146$$

$$= 120 + 55 - 146$$
$$= 175 - 146$$
$$= 29.$$

$$U_2 = 10(12) + \frac{12(12+1)}{2} - 107$$

$$= 120 + 78 - 107$$
$$= 91.$$

Therefore,

$$Z = \frac{29 - \dfrac{10(12)}{2}}{\sqrt{\dfrac{10(12)(10 + 12 + 1)}{12}}}$$

$$= \frac{29 - 60}{\sqrt{230}}$$

$$= \frac{-31}{15.166}$$

$$= -2.044.$$

5. Since $|-2.044| < |\pm 2.581|$, we fail to reject H_0:. We cannot conclude that there is a significant difference between average annual mileage traveled by these two companies.

As the sample sizes become larger, the normal approximation of the U statistic improves; however, if either sample size is < 10, the exact method for calculating the Mann-Whitney U statistic must be employed. This exact technique is beyond the scope of the material presented herein. Also, when there are tied observations within the rankings, they must be handled differently. A more advanced nonparametric statistics textbook will cover both of these topics.

13.6 KRUSKAL-WALLIS ONE-WAY ANALYSIS OF VARIANCE

In Chapter 2, we introduced the analysis of variance and looked at a number of different models, all having a number of assumptions. The Kruskal-Wallis Test is the nonparametric counterpart dealing with the testing of a single factor over two or more independent samples when the data are at least ordinal scaled and when the assumptions required of the more sophisticated models cannot be verified or assumed to be true.

The procedure for calculating the Kruskal-Wallis H statistic is very similar to that outlined for the Mann-Whitney U test. That is, the observations within the k samples must be ranked collectively, but the ranks are summed individually. Once this is done, the equation for calculating H is:

$$H = \frac{12}{N(N+1)} \sum_{i=1}^{k} \frac{R_i^2}{n_i} - 3(N+1)$$

where: N = total sample size ($N = n_1 + n_2 + \cdots + n_k$),
R_i = sum of the ranks of the ith sample,
n_i = sample size of the ith sample,
k = number of samples being tested.

The H statistic follows, approximately, the chi-square distribution with $df = k - 1$, as long as each sample consists of at least five observations. It does not require that these samples be selected from normally distributed populations.

EXAMPLE:

Employee attitude surveys are given to a number of randomly selected employees in each of four plants in order to determine if a significant difference exists in the attitudes of the employees among these plants. The attitude score measurements collected are shown below.

Plant 1	Plant 2	Plant 3	Plant 4
80	100	97	76
65	75	52	95
93	90	86	85
50	59	45	51
96	98	70	46
	83		30

Test at the .05 level of significance in order to determine if a significant difference exists in employee attitude scores among these plants.

SOLUTION:

1. $H_0: \mu_1 = \mu_2 = \mu_3 = \mu_4$

H_1: some inequality does exist

2. $n_1 = 5$

$n_2 = 6$

$n_3 = 5$

$$n_4 = 6$$
$$N = 22$$
$$\alpha = .05$$

3. The chi-square distribution is appropriate here since each value of n_i is ≥ 5.

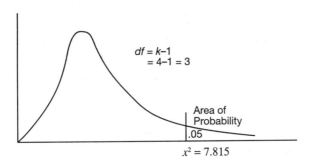

$df = k-1$
$= 4-1 = 3$

Area of
Probability
.05

$x^2 = 7.815$

Therefore, $x^2 = 7.815$.

4. We must rank collectively the scores from the four samples and sum these ranks individually.

Plant 1	Rank	Plant 2	Rank	Plant 3	Rank	Plant 4	Rank
80	12	100	22	97	20	76	11
65	8	75	10	52	6	95	18
93	17	90	16	86	15	85	14
50	4	59	7	45	2	51	5
96	19	98	21	70	9	46	3
	$R_1 = 60$	83	13		$R_3 = 52$	30	1
			$R_2 = 89$				$R_4 = 52$

$$H = \frac{12}{22(22+1)} \left[\frac{(60)^2}{5} + \frac{(89)^2}{6} + \frac{(52)^2}{5} + \frac{(52)^2}{6} \right] - 3(22+1)$$

$$= \frac{12}{506} + \left(\frac{3600}{5} + \frac{7921}{6} + \frac{2704}{5} + \frac{2704}{6} \right) - 3(23)$$

$$= 02372(702 + 1320.17 + 540.8 + 450.7) - 69$$

$$= .02372(3031.67) - 69$$

$$= 71.8973$$

$$= 2.8973$$

5. Since 2.8973 < 7.815, we cannot reject H_0. Therefore, we cannot conclude from the information collected that differences exist among the four plants relative to employee attitudes.

Obviously, when working with the Kruskal-Wallis test, some of the observations may be tied for certain ranks. If this is the case, these tied ranks will be assigned just as they were explained in dealing with the Spearman's rank correlations; i.e., all observations involved in the tie will be given the average rank of the slots included. If at least 25% of the observations are involved in ties, the formula for calculating H should contain a correction factor. When this is the case, the following formula is used for the calculation.

$$H = \frac{\frac{12}{N(N+1)} \sum_{i=1}^{k} \frac{R_i^2}{N_i} - 3(N+1)}{1 - \frac{\sum_{i=1}^{j} \left(t_i^3 - t_i\right)}{N^3 - N}}$$

where: t_i = number of tied observations at slot j,

j = number of ties in total group of data.

EXAMPLE:

Cities are often zoned for governmental and planning purposes. In a certain city, the local officials were interested in determining if the size of houses differed among the four zones. Therefore, they randomly selected a number of houses from each zone and determined the number of rooms in the houses. The following data were collected.

Number of Rooms Per House

ZONE 1	ZONE 2	ZONE 3	ZONE 4
11	7	10	6
5	7	10	6
5	9	6	8
6	6	10	6
8	8	8	7
8	10	10	7
8	5	6	6
	9	7	4
		8	5
			3

Test at the .10 level to determine if a significant difference exists.

SOLUTION:

1. H_0: $\mu_1 = \mu_2 = \mu_3 = \mu_4$
   H_1: Some Inequality does exist

2. $n_1 = 7$
   $n_2 = 8$
   $n_3 = 9$
   $n_4 = 10$
   $N = 34$
   $\alpha = .10$

3.

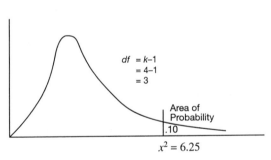

$df = k-1$
$= 4-1$
$= 3$

Area of Probability
.10

$x^2 = 6.25$

Therefore, $x^2 = 6.25$.

Zone 1	Rank	Zone 2	Rank	Zone 3	Rank	Zone 4	Rank
11	34	7	17	10	31	6	10.5
5	4.5	7	17	10	31	6	10.5
5	4.5	9	27.5	6	10.5	8	23
6	10.5	6	10.5	10	31	6	10.5
8	23	8	23	8	23	7	17
8	23	10	31	10	31	7	17
8	23	5	4.5	6	10.5	6	10.5
	$R_1 = 122.5$	9	27.5	7	17	4	2
			$R_2 = 158.0$	8	23	5	4.5
					$R_3 = 208$	3	1
							$R_4 = 106.5$

Since more than 25% of these observations are involved in a tie, H is calculated using the correction factor for ties.

$$H = \frac{\dfrac{12}{34(34+1)}\left[\dfrac{(122.5)^2}{7} + \dfrac{(158.0)^2}{8} + \dfrac{(208)^2}{9} + \dfrac{(106.5)^2}{10}\right] - 3(34+1)}{1 - \dfrac{\left[(4^3-4)+(8^3-8)+(4^3-4)+(7^3-7)+(2^3-2)+(5^3-5)\right]}{34^3 - 34}}$$

$$= \frac{\dfrac{12}{1190}\left[2143.75 + 3120.5 + 4807.1 + 1134.3\right] - 105}{1 - \dfrac{\left[(64-4)+(512-8)+(64-4)+(343-7)+(8-2)+(125-5)\right]}{39304 - 34}}$$

$$= \frac{(.01008)(11205.55) - 105}{1 - \dfrac{1086}{39270}}$$

$$= \frac{7.95144}{1 - .02765}$$

$$= \frac{7.95144}{.9723453}$$

$$= 8.178$$

4. Since 8.178 > 6.25, we reject H_0: and accept H_1:. Therefore, we conclude that there a difference among the four zones relative to the size of houses. Again, however, there is a 10% chance that our conclusion is in error.

Multiple comparisons tests also exist for determining where the differences lie whenever the Kruskal-Wallis test indicates that a difference does exist. These tests are included in advanced nonparametric statistics textbooks.

CHAPTER 14

TIME SERIES ANALYSIS

14.1 COMPONENTS OF A TIME SERIES

A time series involves measurement of some activity over time. The activity may be, for example, sales, income, profit, costs, or population. The time period involved could be daily or weekly, but usually, measurements of business and economic variables are taken monthly, quarterly, or annually. Time series may contain one or more of four types of components which are used to explain variations within the series. These four components are explained below.

1. Trend - The trend component in a time series measures the long-term growth or decline of some activity. Plans for expansion, reduction, and other types of business decisions should be based on projections; therefore, trend analysis is important in making decisions for the future.

2. Seasonal Variations - The seasonal component measures the changes that reoccur at the same time every year; i.e., they may fluctuate with the seasons of the year. Examples of seasonal fluctuations in sales would appear if we were measuring sales of bathing suits, coats, ice cream, swimming pool supplies, etc. Sales of these items would be expected to peak at about the same time year after year. In order to measure this seasonal component, data must be measured on less than an annual basis; usually, seasonal variations are measured either on monthly or quarterly data. Once we have identified the seasonal component, many important decisions may be made relative to size of work force, production scheduling, inventory, etc.

3. Cyclical Fluctuations - The cyclical component measures

209

the fluctuations in a time series that are attributable to fluctuations in the economic indicators, such as interest rates, inflation, and money supply. These fluctuations do not occur in a repetitive pattern as the seasonal variations do; however, they are generally repeated in a long-term pattern, but with varying degrees of intensity. Cyclical fluctuations are difficult to measure outright and are also difficult to predict.

4. Irregular Fluctuations - The irregular component affecting data over time consists of those fluctuations which are not categorized otherwise. They may be the result of extreme weather conditions, earthquakes and other catastrophes, drastic changes in the stock market, or other unpredictable or random factors. As these examples illustrate, the effect of the irregular component may be either positive or negative and certainly may affect different industries and organizations in different ways.

14.2 TREND ANALYSIS

Trend analysis involves the calculation of a trend equation and the plotting of a trend line through a time series. Trend patterns may be linear (straight-line) or curvilinear (exponential or Gompertz type curves). We will discuss only the linear trend pattern, which has a great deal of similarity to the simple linear regression procedure. The main difference which allows for some modification of the equations is the fact that the independent variable is always expressed in some interval of time.

The steps involved in analyzing a trend are:

1. Plot the series of data,
2. Determine which type of line will best fit the average growth or decline of the series,
3. Compute the trend equation,
4. Plot the trend line through the series of data.

The least squares linear trend equation is:

$$Y = a + bX$$

where: Y = the individual values of the data being analyzed,

X = the time interval,

a = the Y intercept, or the value of Y when $X = 0$,

b = the slope of the line, or the per unit change in Y per time period.

If X, the variable which represents time, is coded so that $\Sigma X = 0$, then:

$$a = \frac{\Sigma Y}{n} \qquad\qquad b = \frac{\Sigma XY}{\Sigma x^2}$$

EXAMPLE:

An eleven-year series of sales data was collected from the records of the Bentwood Corporation in order to analyze the trend component in the series. The following data were collected:

Year	Sales ($1,000s)	X=Time	XY	x^2
1979	1,000	-5	-5,000	25
1980	5,000	-4	-20,000	16
1981	7,000	-3	-21,000	9
1982	8,000	-2	-16,000	4
1983	14,000	-1	-14,000	1
1984	18,000	0	0	0
1985	23,000	1	23,000	1
1986	23,000	2	46,000	4
1987	23,000	3	69,000	9
1988	33,000	4	132,000	16
1989	45,000	5	225,000	25
	200,000	0	419,000	110

Calculate the linear least squares trend equation.

SOLUTION:

1. Plot the data.

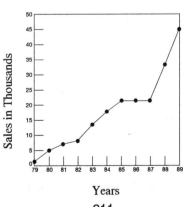

Years

2. We will assume that the best fit to this data is measured by a linear relationship.

3. Since X is coded so that $\Sigma X = 0$, we calculate the trend equation using the simplified formulas for a and b:

$$Y = a + bX$$

$$\hat{Y} = 18,181.8 + 3,809.1X$$

Origin: July 1, 1984

X units: 1 year

Y units: $1,000s

$$a = \frac{\Sigma Y}{n} = \frac{200,000}{11} = 18,181.8$$

$$b = \frac{\Sigma XY}{\Sigma X^2} = \frac{419,000}{110} = 3,809.1$$

The interpretation of this equation is that when $X = 0$ (July 1, 1984, since each coded value for X represents the middle of the year), average sales is $18,181,800 and that sales is increasing an average of $3,809,100 per year (since X units are recorded in years).

4. Since the trend line is a straight line, it can be plotted simply by selecting two values of X and substituting these into the trend equation to solve for Y at these two points.

if $X = -3$; $\hat{Y} = 18,181.8 + 3809.1(-3)$

(1981) $\hat{Y} = 6754.5$

if $X = 3$; $\hat{Y} = 18,181.8 + 3809.1(3)$

(1987) $\hat{Y} = 29609.1$

These values are located on the graph with a straight line drawn through the two points. This results in the chart shown on the following page.

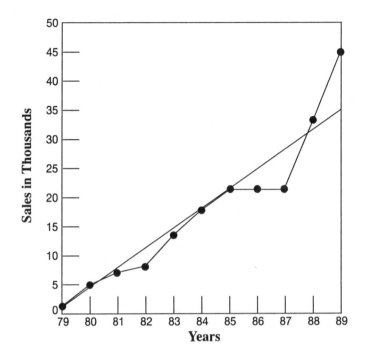

Recall that the equations for calculating a and b require that $\Sigma X = 0$. In the previous example, we were able to meet this requirement since there were an odd number of years (11) and the one in the middle was assigned the value 0, with the years preceding assigned negative values one unit apart and the years following assigned positive values one year apart. But, if there are an even number of years, this method of assigning codes to the years will not work because not only must $X = 0$, there must also be equal distances between the coded values. Therefore, when there is an even number of years, we must use the method of assigning the X codes, which appear in the following example.

EXAMPLE:

Ten years of profit data from Bentwood Corporation are given below. Calculate a least squares linear trend equation.

YEAR	Y-Profit/($1,000s)	X	XY	X²
1980	325	-9	-2925	81
1981	379	-7	-2653	49
1982	398	-5	-1990	25
1983	393	-3	-1179	9

YEAR	Y-Profit/($1,000s)	X	XY	X²
1984	412	-1	-412	1
1985	453	1	453	1
1986	490	3	1470	9
1987	388	5	1940	25
1988	425	7	2975	49
1989	454	9	4086	81
	4117	0	1765	330

$$a = \frac{\Sigma Y}{n} = \frac{4117}{10} = 411.7$$

$$b = \frac{\Sigma XY}{\Sigma X^2} = \frac{1765}{330} = 5.35$$

$$\hat{Y} = 411.7 + 5.35\,X$$

Origin: January 1, 1985

X units: $\frac{1}{2}$ years

Y units: $1,000s

The interpretation is that the average profit as of January 1, 1985 is $411,700 and the average increase every 6 months ($\frac{1}{2}$ year) is $5,350.

Note that the X codes in this example are all old numbers, but that they do meet the coding requirements. That is, $\Sigma X = 0$ and they represent equal units; each is represented by the equidistance of 2 between each X value. Since the Xs are two units apart, each X represents one half year. Note also that the point of origin is different. In the first example, $X = 0$ in the middle of 1984; in this example, the implied location of X is one-half way between the middle of 1984 and the middle of 1985, or January 1, 1985.

If, once we plot the data, we determine that it does not adhere to a constant growth or decline, we must use one of the curvilinear techniques to fit a trend equation. Some of the more common ones that are typically explained in statistics textbooks are the quadratic, the exponential, and the Gompertz curve.

14.3 SEASONAL VARIATIONS

The magnitude of the fluctuations in a series of data that reoccur at approximately the same time each year can be measured by determining a seasonal index using past data. A seasonal index is typically computed on data which are collected either on a quarterly basis or on a monthly basis. The procedure involves the moving total and moving average concepts as outlined below.

1. Compute either 4-quarter or 12-month moving totals, centering each in the middle of the period it represents.

2. Compute a 2-year moving total for each quarter or month resulting in the total of the 2 years of data being centered at the same point in time as the original data.

3. Compute moving averages by dividing the 2-year totals by 8 for quarterly data or by 24 for monthly data.

4. Divide each original value by its moving average and multiply each by 100 to form the "ratio-to-moving-average" percentages.

5. Average the quarterly or monthly "ratio-to-moving-average" to arrive at a seasonal index value for each quarter or month.

EXAMPLE:

Quarterly sales are given below. Calculate the seasonal index.

SOLUTION:

Following the five steps outlined below, we will set up our work in a tabular format as follows:

1. Four-quarter moving totals are calculated and presented in Column 4 of the table. The first moving total is 375 (68 + 90 + 106 + 111); since it represents the sum over the year 1984, it is centered in the middle of the year (July 1, 1984), which is the reason that the value 375 is centered between the second and third quarters. Moving totals from that point are determined by subtracting the figure on the top and picking up the next figure — always including the sum of four numbers.

2. Since each 4-quarter moving total is centered at the beginning of the quarter and the original sales are centered in the

215

middle of the quarter, the 8-quarter moving totals (which are the sum of two quarter moving totals) are calculated in order to bring the moving totals back in line with the original sales data. The 8-quarter moving total which represents the third quarter is 743 and is the sum of 375 and 368; 728 is the sum of 368 and 360, etc.

3. In column 6, the moving averages are determined by dividing each 8-quarter moving total by 8. Note that these figures are reflecting the same point in time as the original data due to the step of computing 8-quarter moving totals in column 5.

4. Ratios to moving averages are then calculated (column 7) by dividing the original sales figures from column 3 by the corresponding moving averages (column 6) with the decimal shifted two places to the right to reflect these values as percentages ($106/92.9 \times 100 = 114.1$; $111/91 \times 100 = 122.0$; et cetera).

5. Here we take the ratios from column 7 and group them by the quarter they represent and obtain an average per quarter by adding the ratios and dividing by the number of ratios representing each quarter. This procedure is easier to accomplish if we set these ratios up in a tabular format reflecting each quarter.

(1) Year	(2) Qt	(3) Sales($1,000s)	(4) 4-Qt Moving Total	(5) 8-Qt Moving Total	(6) Moving Average	(7) Ratio To Moving Average
1984	1	68				
	2	90				
	3	106	375	743	92.9	114.1
	4	111	368	728	91.0	122.0
1985	1	61	360	717	89.6	68.1
	2	82	357	719	89.9	91.2
	3	103	362	730	91.3	112.8
	4	116	368	742	92.8	125.0
1986	1	67	374	753	94.1	71.2
	2	88	379	764	95.5	92.1
	3	108	285	772	96.6	111.8
	4	122	388	777	97.1	125.6
1987	1	70	389	780	97.5	71.8
	2	89	391	772	96.5	92.2
	3	110	381	756	94.5	116.4
	4	112	375	730	91.3	122.7

(1) Year	(2) Qt	(3) Sales($1,000s)	(4) 4-Qt Moving Total	(5) 8-Qt Moving Total	(6) Moving Average	(7) Ratio To Moving Average
1988	1	64	355	698	87.3	73.3
	2	69	343	686	85.7	80.5
	3	98	350	693	86.6	113.2
	4	112	352	702	87.8	127.6
1989	1	71	357	709	88.6	80.1
	2	71	369	726	90.8	78.2
	3	103				
	4	124				

Quarter 1	Quarter 2	Quarter 3	Quarter 4
		114.1	122.0
68.1	91.2	112.8	125.0
71.2	92.1	111.8	125.6
71.8	92.2	116.4	122.7
73.3	80.5	113.2	127.6
80.1	78.2		
364.5	434.2	568.3	622.9

Seasonal Index
Quarter 1 – 364.5/5 = 72.9
Quarter 2 – 434.2/5 = 86.8
Quarter 3 – 568.3/5 = 113.7
Quarter 4 – 622.9/5 = 124.6

In order to interpret the meaning of these values, we compare each with the value of 100. If the index is below 100, it represents that the series has a seasonal impact for that period which is below normal; the amount below normal is determined by the magnitude of the difference between the index number and 100. If the index is greater than 100, the difference between the value and 100 reflects the "above normal" seasonal impact. If there were no seasonal fluctuations within the data series, the seasonal index for each quarter would be 100.

The seasonal index for this example indicates that, on the average, sales are 27.1% (100% – 72.9%) below normal in quarter 1; 13.2% below normal in quarter 2; 13.7% above normal in quarter 3; and 24.6% above normal in quarter 4. Since sales are almost 50% greater in the last half of the year than in the first half, plans should be made to best fit resources, personnel, and advertising to this pattern.

14.4 CYCLICAL FLUCTUATIONS

Cyclical fluctuations, those which may be attributable to changes in major economic indicators and which do not reoccur in a consistent manner, are not measured directly, but are isolated from a series by removing those fluctuations which can be measured directly. The procedure involves the use of trend effects and seasonal effects in the isolation process. The technique to use depends on whether the series is annual data, or less-than-annual data.

Annual Data

If data are collected annually, no seasonal variations can be detected. However, annual data may possess trend effects (T), cyclical fluctuations (C), and irregular fluctuations (I). In other words we may think of the data in this way.

$$Y = T \times C \times I$$

That is, each data value is a function of the multiplicative effect of these three individual components. In order to attempt to isolate the cyclical fluctuations, we divide through by the effect of trend, which, as we have seen, we can measure. This leaves the following:

$$Y = \frac{T \times C \times I}{T}$$

$$Y = C \times I$$

We are left with not only cyclical effects, but irregular effects as well. Since irregular fluctuations cannot be measured directly, they are usually either assumed away, or if a particular situation occurred of which knowledge of the impact is available, this irregular fluctuation may be removed from the series by dividing through by this information as follows:

$$Y = \frac{C \times I}{I} = C.$$

To illustrate this concept, the example used for analyzing a trend will be used.

EXAMPLE:

Using the sales of the Bentwood Corporation previously studied, isolate the cyclical fluctuation from the data. Assume that no irregular fluctuations exist.

(1) Year	(2) X	(3) Y-Sales/($1,000s)	(4) Y-Trend Value(T)	(5) Y/T * 100
1979	-5	1,000	-8,63.7	111.9
1980	-4	5,000	2,945.4	169.8
1981	-3	7,000	6,754.5	103.6
1982	-2	8,000	10,563.6	75.7
1983	-1	14,000	14,372.7	97.4
1984	0	18,000	18,181.8	99.0
1985	1	23,000	21,990.9	104.6
1986	2	23,000	25,800.0	89.1
1987	3	23,000	29,609.1	77.7
1988	4	33,000	33,418.2	98.7
1989	5	48,000	37,227.3	128.9

SOLUTION:

1. In order to isolate the cyclical fluctuations, a trend value for each year must be determined. These values will be determined by using the trend equation previously calculated:

$$\hat{Y} = 18,181.8 + 3809.1X$$

Origin: July 1, 1984

X units: 1 year

Y units: $1,000s

and substituting the value of X for each year into the equation. For example,

1979 – X = -5; $\hat{Y} = 18,181.8 + 3809.1(-5)$

$\hat{Y} = 18,181.8 - 19045.5$

$\hat{Y} = -863.7$

1980 – X = -4; $\hat{Y} = 18,181.8 + 3809.1(-4)$

$$\hat{Y} = 18{,}181.8 - 15236.4$$

$$\hat{Y} = 2945.4$$

as shown in column 4 - Trend Values.

2. To isolate the cyclical effects from this sales series, original sales figures from column 3 are divided by the trend values from column 4 and multiplied by 100, shifting the decimal two places to the right to express the results as percentages:

$(1000/-863.7 \times 100 = 111.9; 5000/2945.4 \times 100 = 169.8$, etc.).

3. The resulting values shown in column 5 reflect the cyclical effects in the series. As with the seasonal indexes, the amounts that these values differ from 100 indicate the magnitude of the cyclical fluctuations. The duration of the cycle is noted by observing the length of time involved from peak-to-peak or low-point-to-low-point.

For example, if the values which have been adjusted are plotted, we can observe the cyclical fluctuations.

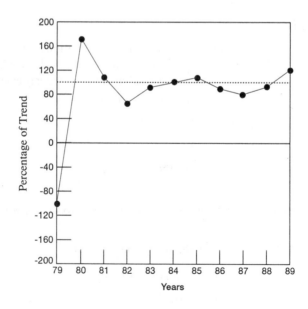

Less-than-Annual Data

When data are less-than-annual, usually either monthly or quarterly, and when seasonal variations exist in the series as well as trend variations, we must remove the effect of both of these if we are to isolate the cyclical fluctuations. Therefore,

$$Y = \frac{T \times S \times C \times I}{T \times S}$$

$$= C \times I,$$

and again, we must either assume away any irregular fluctuations or, if they can be measured, do so, and divide through by these effects as well, leaving:

$$Y = \frac{C \times I}{I}$$

$$Y = C$$

The procedure and the form of output will be as we have just discussed for the annual data situation. However, monthly or quarterly trend values must be determined rather than annual trend values. This may be accomplished by the same method as outlined earlier. The only difference will be that the time intervals reflect smaller periods.

14.5 IRREGULAR FLUCTUATIONS

Irregular fluctuations, as previously defined, are those occurrences which affect a series of data over time such as "acts of God," wars, strikes, or fires. These are not generally measurable nor are they predictable. These fluctuations are typically ignored when analyzing time series unless those analyzing the data believe that they have the background or expertise to approximate the effect of an irregular event.

14.6 INDEX NUMBERS

Index numbers are used as a means of comparing a number of periods of data with one particular value for some specified period (base period). The purpose of this comparison is to determine how much growth or decline is evident in each of the periods when compared with the period which has been specified as the base period. The procedure is simple; the value for each period is divided by the value for the base period and multiplied by

100. The amount under or over 100 reflects the growth or decline in the series when compared to the base period.

EXAMPLE:

Year	Y-Profit ($1,000s)	Index (Base = 1980) Numbers
1980	325	100.0
1981	379	116.6
1982	398	122.5
1983	393	120.9
1984	412	126.8
1985	453	139.4
1986	490	150.8
1987	388	119.4
1988	425	130.8
1989	454	139.7

SOLUTION:

If we set 1980 as the base period, we simply divide the profit for each year by 325 and multiply by 100 for the percentage notation: ($325/325 \times 100 = 100.0$; $379/325 \times 100 = 116.6$; $398/325 \times 100 = 122.5$, etc.). These values reflect the change in profit for each year as compared to 1980. For example, profits increased 50.8% from 1980 to 1986; profits also increased by 39.7% from 1980 to 1989.

If, for example, we were interested in determining the change in profit from year to year, we would work with a revolving base period, where the profit for each year is compared with the profit of the preceding year ($379/325 \times 100 = 116.6$; $398/379 \times 100 = 105.0$; $393/398 \times 100 = 98.7$, etc.).

Year	Y-Profit ($1,000s)	Moving Base Index Numbers
1980	325	–
1981	379	116.6
1982	398	105.0
1983	393	98.7
1984	412	104.8
1985	453	110.0
1986	490	108.2
1987	388	79.2
1988	425	109.5
1989	454	106.8

This information indicates that in only two years was the profit less than what it had been the previous year. In 1983, profits were down 1.3% from

1982, and in 1987, profits were down 20.8% from the preceding year, 1986.

The base period may be any year within the data set. However, we must be careful that the conditions in the period selected as the base are "normal." That is, we should not use a period of recession or any other period in which abnormal economic conditions existed. It is also appropriate, if desired, to use the average of the values of a number of periods for the base value.

The most familiar governmental index numbers are the Consumer Price Index, which is a measure of the overall change in prices of goods and services; the Wholesale Price Index, which is a measure of change of the prices in goods sold in the wholesale market; and the Dow-Jones Industrial Average stock market index.

14.7 FORECASTING

Forecasting is the process of predicting the future. It is through various forecasting techniques that we are able to predict; e.g., future sales in light of changes in advertising, plant expansion needs, or many other business related types of decisions. Obviously, we should not make decisions involving large investments without having some idea as to what the future holds. Forecasting techniques are usually categorized as either judgmental (or subjective) methods, or as quantitative techniques that involve statistical methodology.

Judgmental or subjective forecasting methods rely on information from those having expertise relative to the particular issue at hand. The brains of these individuals are picked for their judgment or feelings as to what might happen if certain changes are made within an organization; generally, top management is included as well as the sales force and others with the desired expertise. Many long-term decisions are made from information collected from consumers through surveys, focus groups, or just conversation. Consultants are often used to assist in predicting possible outcomes based on current conditions and potential changes.

Statistical forecasting techniques involve formal models which incorporate past and current data to predict what will happen in the future. Regression analysis and time series analysis are two methods which we have previously introduced that are useful in forecasting. We can extend or extrapolate both a regression relationship and a time series to predict the changes that will be expected to take place under certain conditions. Other statistical forecasting techniques which haven't been introduced involve moving averages and smoothing techniques and the more advanced Box-Jenkins method.

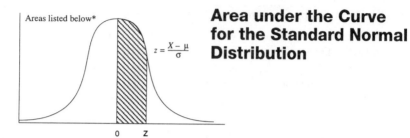

Area under the Curve for the Standard Normal Distribution

Areas listed below*

$z = \dfrac{X - \mu}{\sigma}$

0   z

Z	.00	.01	.02	.03	.04	.05	.06	.07	.08	.09
0.0	.0000	.0040	.0080	.0120	.0160	.0199	.0239	.0279	.0319	.0359
0.1	.0398	.0438	.0478	.0517	.0557	.0596	.0636	.0675	.0714	.0753
0.2	.0793	.0832	.0871	.0910	.0948	.0987	.1026	.1064	.1103	.1141
0.3	.1179	.1217	.1255	.1293	.1331	.1368	.1406	.1443	.1480	.1517
0.4	.1554	.1591	.1628	.1664	.1700	.1736	.1772	.1808	.1844	.1879
0.5	.1915	.1950	.1985	.2019	.2054	.2088	.2123	.2157	.2190	.2224
0.6	.2257	.2291	.2324	.2357	.2389	.2422	.2454	.2486	.2518	.2549
0.7	.2580	.2612	.2642	.2673	.2704	.2734	.2764	.2794	.2823	.2852
0.8	.2881	.2910	.2939	.2967	.2995	.3023	.3051	.3078	.3106	.3133
0.9	.3159	.3186	.3212	.3238	.3264	.3289	.3315	.3340	.3365	.3389
1.0	.3413	.3438	.3461	.3485	.3508	.3531	.3554	.3577	.3599	.3621
1.1	.3643	.3665	.3686	.3708	.3729	.3749	.3770	.3790	.3810	.3830
1.2	.3849	.3869	.3888	.3907	.3925	.3944	.3962	.3980	.3997	.4014
1.3	.4032	.4049	.4066	.4082	.4099	.4115	.4131	.4147	.4162	.4177
1.4	.4192	.4207	.4222	.4236	.4251	.4265	.4279	.4292	.4306	.4319
1.5	.4332	.4345	.4357	.4370	.4382	.4394	.4406	.4418	.4429	.4441
1.6	.4452	.4463	.4474	.4484	.4495	.4505	.4515	.4525	.4535	.4545
1.7	.4554	.4564	.4573	.4582	.4591	.4599	.4608	.4616	.4625	.4633
1.8	.4641	.4649	.4656	.4664	.4671	.4678	.4686	.4693	.4699	.4706
1.9	.4713	.4719	.4726	.4732	.4738	.4744	.4750	.4756	.4761	.4767
2.0	.4772	.4778	.4783	.4788	.4793	.4798	.4803	.4808	.4812	.4817
2.1	.4821	.4826	.4830	.4834	.4838	.4842	.4846	.4850	.4854	.4857
2.2	.4861	.4864	.4868	.4871	.4875	.4878	.4881	.4884	.4887	.4890
2.3	.4893	.4896	.4898	.4901	.4904	.4906	.4909	.4911	.4913	.4916
2.4	.4918	.4920	.4922	.4925	.4927	.4929	.4931	.4932	.4934	.4936
2.5	.4938	.4940	.4941	.4943	.4945	.4946	.4948	.4949	.4951	.4952
2.6	.4953	.4955	.4956	.4957	.4959	.4960	.4961	.4962	.4963	.4964
2.7	.4965	.4966	.4967	.4968	.4969	.4970	.4971	.4972	.4973	.4974
2.8	.4974	.4975	.4976	.4977	.4977	.4978	.4979	.4979	.4980	.4981
2.9	.4981	.4982	.4983	.4983	.4984	.4984	.4985	.4985	.4986	.4986
3.0	.4987									
3.5	.4997									
4.0	.4999									

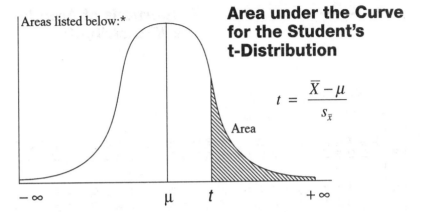

Area under the Curve for the Student's t-Distribution

Areas listed below:*

$$t = \frac{\overline{X} - \mu}{s_{\overline{x}}}$$

Area

$-\infty$ $\quad$ μ $\quad$ t $\quad$ $+\infty$

df	0.10	0.05	0.025	0.01	0.005
1	3.07	6.314	12.706	31.821	63.657
2	1.886	2.920	4.303	6.965	9.925
3	1.638	2.353	3.182	4.541	5.841
4	1.533	2.132	2.776	3.747	4.604
5	1.476	2.015	2.571	3.365	4.032
6	1.440	1.943	2.447	3.143	3.707
7	1.415	1.895	2.365	2.998	3.499
8	1.397	1.860	2.306	2.896	3.355
9	1.383	1.833	2.262	2.821	3.250
10	1.372	1.812	2.228	2.764	3.169
11	1.363	1.796	2.201	2.718	3.106
12	1.356	1.782	2.179	2.681	3.055
13	1.350	1.771	2.160	2.650	3.012
14	1.345	1.761	2.145	2.624	2.977
15	1.341	1.753	2.131	2.602	2.947
16	1.337	1.746	2.120	2.583	2.921
17	1.333	1.740	2.110	2.567	2.898
18	1.330	1.734	2.101	2.552	2.878
19	1.328	1.729	2.093	2.539	2.861
20	1.325	1.725	2.086	2.528	2.845
21	1.323	1.721	2.080	2.518	2.831
22	1.321	1.717	2.074	2.508	2.819
23	1.319	1.714	2.069	2.500	2.807
24	1.318	1.711	2.064	2.492	2.797
25	1.316	1.708	2.060	2.485	2.787
26	1.315	1.706	2.056	2.479	2.779
27	1.314	1.703	2.052	2.473	2.771
28	1.313	1.701	2.048	2.467	2.763
29	1.311	1.699	2.045	2.462	2.756
30	1.310	1.697	2.042	2.457	2.750
40	1.303	1.684	2.021	2.423	2.704
60	1.296	1.671	2.000	2.390	2.660
120	1.289	1.658	1.980	2.358	2.617
∞	1.282	1.645	1.960	2.326	2.576

225

Areas listed below:

For *df* = 1.2   For *df* ≥ 30

Proportions of Area for the X^2 Distribution

df	0.995	0.090	0.975	0.950	0.900	0.500	0.100	0.050	0.025	0.010	0.005
1	0.00004	0.00016	0.0009	0.00393	0.0158	0.455	2.71	3.84	5.02	6.63	7.88
2	0.0100	0.0201	0.0506	0.103	0.211	1.386	4.61	5.99	7.38	9.21	10.60
3	0.072	0.115	0.216	0.352	0.584	2.366	6.25	7.81	9.35	11.34	12.84
4	0.207	0.297	0.484	0.711	1.064	3.357	7.78	9.49	11.14	13.28	14.86
5	0.412	0.554	0.831	1.145	1.61	4.251	9.24	11.07	12.83	15.09	16.75
6	0.676	0.872	1.24	1.64	2.20	5.35	10.64	12.59	14.45	16.81	18.55
7	0.989	1.24	1.69	2.17	2.83	6.35	12.02	14.07	16.01	18.48	20.28
8	1.34	1.65	2.18	2.73	3.49	7.34	13.36	15.51	17.53	20.09	21.96
9	1.73	2.09	2.70	3.33	4.17	8.34	14.68	16.92	19.02	21.67	23.59
10	2.16	2.56	3.25	3.94	4.87	9.34	15.99	18.31	20.48	23.21	25.19
11	2.60	3.05	3.82	4.57	5.58	10.34	17.28	19.68	21.92	24.73	26.76
12	3.07	3.57	4.40	5.23	6.30	11.34	18.55	21.03	23.34	26.22	28.30
13	3.57	4.11	5.01	5.89	7.04	12.34	19.81	22.36	24.74	27.69	29.82
14	4.07	4.66	5.63	6.57	7.79	13.34	21.06	23.68	26.12	29.14	31.32
15	4.60	5.23	6.26	7.26	8.55	14.34	22.31	25.00	27.49	30.58	32.80
16	5.14	5.81	6.91	7.96	9.31	15.34	23.51	26.30	28.85	32.00	34.27
17	5.70	6.41	7.56	8.67	10.09	16.34	24.77	27.59	30.19	33.41	35.72
18	6.26	7.01	8.23	9.39	10.86	17.34	25.99	28.87	31.53	34.81	37.16
19	6.84	7.63	8.91	10.12	10.65	18.34	27.20	30.14	32.85	36.19	38.58
20	7.43	8.26	9.59	10.85	12.44	19.34	28.41	31.41	34.17	37.57	40.00
21	8.03	8.90	10.28	11.59	13.24	20.34	29.62	32.67	35.4	38.93	41.40
22	8.64	9.54	10.98	12.34	14.04	21.34	30.81	33.92	36.78	40.29	42.80
23	9.26	10.20	11.69	13.09	14.85	22.34	32.01	35.17	38.08	41.64	44.18
24	9.89	10.86	12.40	13.85	15.66	23.34	33.20	36.42	39.36	42.98	45.56
25	10.52	11.52	13.12	14.61	16.47	24.34	34.38	37.65	40.65	44.31	46.93

df	0.995	0.090	0.975	0.950	0.900	0.500	0.100	0.050	0.025	0.010	0.005
26	11.16	12.20	13.84	15.38	17.29	25.34	35.56	38.89	41.92	45.64	48.29
27	11.81	12.83	14.57	16.15	18.11	26.34	36.74	40.11	43.19	46.96	49.64
28	12.46	13.56	15.31	19.93	18.94	27.34	37.92	41.34	44.46	48.28	50.99
29	13.12	14.26	16.05	17.71	19.77	28.34	39.09	42.56	45.72	49.59	52.34
30	13.79	14.95	16.79	18.49	20.60	29.34	40.26	43.77	46.98	50.89	53.67
40	20.71	22.16	24.43	26.51	29.05	39.34	51.81	55.76	59.34	63.69	66.77
50	27.99	29.71	32.36	34.76	37.69	49.33	63.17	67.50	71.42	76.15	79.49
60	35.53	37.43	40.48	43.19	46.46	59.33	74.40	79.08	83.30	88.38	91.95
70	43.28	45.44	48.76	51.74	55.33	69.33	85.33	90.53	95.02	100.40	104.20
80	51.17	53.44	51.17	60.39	64.28	79.33	98.58	101.90	106.60	112.30	116.30
90	59.20	61.75	65.65	69.13	73.29	89.33	107.60	113.10	118.10	124.10	128.30
100	67.33	70.06	74.22	77.93	83.36	99.33	118.50	124.30	129.60	135.80	140.20

Critical Values of F (Probabilities of 5 and 1 Percent)

degrees of freedom (numerator)

Each cell lists the 5% critical value (top) and the 1% critical value (bottom, bold).

den. df	1	2	3	4	5	6	7	8	9	10	11	12	14	16	20	24	30	40	50	75	100	200	500	∞
1	161 / 4,052	200 / 4,999	216 / 5,403	225 / 5,625	230 / 5,764	234 / 5,859	237 / 5,928	239 / 5,981	241 / 6,022	242 / 6,056	243 / 6,082	244 / 6,106	245 / 6,142	246 / 6,169	248 / 6,208	249 / 6,234	250 / 6,261	251 / 6,286	252 / 6,302	253 / 6,323	253 / 6,334	254 / 6,352	254 / 6,361	254 / 6,366
2	18.51 / 98.49	19.00 / 99.00	19.16 / 99.17	19.25 / 99.25	19.30 / 99.30	19.33 / 99.33	19.36 / 99.36	19.37 / 99.37	19.38 / 99.39	19.39 / 99.40	19.40 / 99.41	19.41 / 99.42	19.42 / 99.43	19.43 / 99.44	19.44 / 99.45	19.45 / 99.46	19.46 / 99.47	19.47 / 99.48	19.47 / 99.48	19.48 / 99.49	19.49 / 99.49	19.49 / 99.49	19.50 / 99.50	19.50 / 99.50
3	10.13 / 34.12	9.55 / 30.82	9.28 / 29.46	9.12 / 28.71	9.01 / 28.24	8.94 / 27.91	8.88 / 27.67	8.84 / 27.49	8.81 / 27.34	8.78 / 27.23	8.76 / 27.13	8.74 / 27.05	8.71 / 26.92	8.69 / 26.83	8.66 / 26.69	8.64 / 26.60	8.62 / 26.50	8.60 / 26.41	8.58 / 26.35	8.57 / 26.27	8.56 / 26.23	8.54 / 26.18	8.54 / 26.14	8.53 / 26.12
4	7.71 / 21.20	6.94 / 18.00	6.59 / 16.69	6.39 / 15.98	6.26 / 15.52	6.16 / 15.21	6.09 / 14.98	6.04 / 14.80	6.00 / 14.66	5.96 / 14.54	5.93 / 14.45	5.91 / 14.37	5.87 / 14.24	5.84 / 14.15	5.80 / 14.02	5.77 / 13.93	5.74 / 13.83	5.71 / 13.74	5.70 / 13.69	5.68 / 13.61	5.66 / 13.57	5.65 / 13.52	5.64 / 13.48	5.63 / 13.46
5	6.61 / 16.26	5.79 / 13.27	5.41 / 12.06	5.19 / 11.39	5.05 / 10.97	4.95 / 10.67	4.88 / 10.45	4.82 / 10.29	4.78 / 10.15	4.74 / 10.05	4.70 / 9.96	4.68 / 9.89	4.64 / 9.77	4.60 / 9.68	4.56 / 9.55	4.53 / 9.47	4.50 / 9.38	4.46 / 9.29	4.44 / 9.24	4.42 / 9.17	4.40 / 9.13	4.38 / 9.07	4.37 / 9.04	4.36 / 9.02
6	5.99 / 13.74	5.14 / 10.92	4.76 / 9.78	4.53 / 9.15	4.39 / 8.75	4.28 / 8.47	4.21 / 8.26	4.15 / 8.10	4.10 / 7.98	4.06 / 7.87	4.03 / 7.79	4.00 / 7.72	3.96 / 7.60	3.92 / 7.52	3.87 / 7.39	3.84 / 7.31	3.81 / 7.23	3.77 / 7.14	3.75 / 7.09	3.72 / 7.02	3.71 / 6.99	3.69 / 6.94	3.68 / 6.90	3.67 / 6.88
7	5.59 / 12.25	4.74 / 9.55	4.34 / 8.45	4.12 / 7.85	3.97 / 7.46	3.87 / 7.19	3.79 / 7.00	3.73 / 6.84	3.68 / 6.71	3.63 / 6.62	3.60 / 6.54	3.57 / 6.47	3.52 / 6.35	3.49 / 6.27	3.44 / 6.15	3.41 / 6.07	3.38 / 5.98	3.34 / 5.90	3.32 / 5.85	3.29 / 5.78	3.28 / 5.75	3.25 / 5.70	3.24 / 5.67	3.23 / 5.65
8	5.32 / 11.26	4.46 / 8.65	4.07 / 7.59	3.84 / 7.01	3.69 / 6.63	3.58 / 6.37	3.50 / 6.19	3.44 / 6.03	3.39 / 5.91	3.34 / 5.82	3.31 / 5.74	3.28 / 5.67	3.23 / 5.56	3.20 / 5.48	3.15 / 5.36	3.12 / 5.28	3.08 / 5.20	3.05 / 5.11	3.03 / 5.06	3.00 / 5.00	2.98 / 4.96	2.96 / 4.91	2.94 / 4.88	2.93 / 4.86
9	5.12 / 10.56	4.26 / 8.02	3.86 / 6.99	3.63 / 6.42	3.48 / 6.06	3.37 / 5.80	3.29 / 5.62	3.23 / 5.47	3.18 / 5.35	3.13 / 5.26	3.10 / 5.18	3.07 / 5.11	3.02 / 5.00	2.98 / 4.92	2.93 / 4.80	2.90 / 4.73	2.86 / 4.64	2.82 / 4.56	2.80 / 4.51	2.77 / 4.45	2.76 / 4.41	2.73 / 4.36	2.72 / 4.33	2.71 / 4.31
10	4.96 / 10.04	4.10 / 7.56	3.71 / 6.55	3.48 / 5.99	3.33 / 5.64	3.22 / 5.39	3.14 / 5.21	3.07 / 5.06	3.02 / 4.95	2.97 / 4.85	2.94 / 4.78	2.91 / 4.71	2.86 / 4.60	2.82 / 4.52	2.77 / 4.41	2.74 / 4.33	2.70 / 4.25	2.67 / 4.17	2.64 / 4.12	2.61 / 4.05	2.59 / 4.01	2.56 / 3.96	2.55 / 3.93	2.54 / 3.91
11	4.84 / 9.65	3.98 / 7.20	3.59 / 6.22	3.36 / 5.67	3.20 / 5.32	3.09 / 5.07	3.01 / 4.88	2.95 / 4.74	2.90 / 4.63	2.86 / 4.54	2.82 / 4.46	2.79 / 4.40	2.74 / 4.29	2.70 / 4.21	2.65 / 4.10	2.61 / 4.02	2.57 / 3.94	2.53 / 3.86	2.50 / 3.80	2.47 / 3.74	2.45 / 3.70	2.42 / 3.66	2.41 / 3.62	2.40 / 3.60
12	4.75 / 9.33	3.88 / 6.93	3.49 / 5.95	3.26 / 5.41	3.11 / 5.06	3.00 / 4.82	2.92 / 4.65	2.85 / 4.50	2.80 / 4.39	2.76 / 4.30	2.72 / 4.22	2.69 / 4.16	2.64 / 4.05	2.60 / 3.98	2.54 / 3.86	2.50 / 3.78	2.46 / 3.70	2.42 / 3.61	2.40 / 3.56	2.36 / 3.49	2.35 / 3.46	2.32 / 3.41	2.31 / 3.38	2.30 / 3.36
13	4.67 / 9.07	3.80 / 6.70	3.41 / 5.74	3.18 / 5.20	3.02 / 4.86	2.92 / 4.62	2.84 / 4.44	2.77 / 4.30	2.72 / 4.19	2.67 / 4.10	2.63 / 4.02	2.60 / 3.96	2.55 / 3.85	2.51 / 3.78	2.46 / 3.67	2.42 / 3.59	2.38 / 3.51	2.34 / 3.42	2.32 / 3.37	2.28 / 3.30	2.26 / 3.27	2.24 / 3.21	2.22 / 3.18	2.21 / 3.16
14	4.60 / 8.86	3.74 / 6.51	3.34 / 5.56	3.11 / 5.03	2.96 / 4.69	2.85 / 4.46	2.77 / 4.28	2.70 / 4.14	2.65 / 4.03	2.60 / 3.94	2.56 / 3.86	2.53 / 3.80	2.48 / 3.70	2.44 / 3.62	2.39 / 3.51	2.35 / 3.43	2.31 / 3.34	2.27 / 3.26	2.24 / 3.21	2.21 / 3.14	2.19 / 3.11	2.16 / 3.06	2.14 / 3.02	2.13 / 3.00
15	4.54 / 8.68	3.68 / 6.36	3.29 / 5.42	3.06 / 4.89	2.90 / 4.56	2.79 / 4.32	2.70 / 4.14	2.64 / 4.00	2.59 / 3.89	2.55 / 3.80	2.51 / 3.73	2.48 / 3.67	2.43 / 3.56	2.39 / 3.48	2.33 / 3.36	2.29 / 3.29	2.25 / 3.20	2.21 / 3.12	2.18 / 3.07	2.15 / 3.00	2.12 / 2.97	2.10 / 2.92	2.08 / 2.89	2.07 / 2.87
16	4.49 / 8.53	3.63 / 6.23	3.24 / 5.29	3.01 / 4.77	2.85 / 4.44	2.74 / 4.20	2.66 / 4.03	2.59 / 3.89	2.54 / 3.78	2.49 / 3.69	2.45 / 3.61	2.42 / 3.55	2.37 / 3.45	2.33 / 3.37	2.28 / 3.25	2.24 / 3.18	2.20 / 3.10	2.16 / 3.01	2.13 / 2.96	2.09 / 2.89	2.07 / 2.86	2.04 / 2.80	2.02 / 2.77	2.01 / 2.75
17	4.45 / 8.40	3.59 / 6.11	3.20 / 5.18	2.96 / 4.67	2.81 / 4.34	2.70 / 4.10	2.62 / 3.93	2.55 / 3.79	2.50 / 3.68	2.45 / 3.59	2.41 / 3.52	2.38 / 3.45	2.33 / 3.35	2.29 / 3.27	2.23 / 3.16	2.19 / 3.08	2.15 / 3.00	2.11 / 2.92	2.08 / 2.86	2.04 / 2.79	2.02 / 2.76	1.99 / 2.70	1.97 / 2.67	1.96 / 2.65
18	4.41 / 8.28	3.55 / 6.01	3.16 / 5.09	2.93 / 4.58	2.77 / 4.25	2.66 / 4.01	2.58 / 3.85	2.51 / 3.71	2.46 / 3.60	2.41 / 3.51	2.37 / 3.44	2.34 / 3.37	2.29 / 3.27	2.25 / 3.19	2.19 / 3.07	2.15 / 3.00	2.11 / 2.91	2.07 / 2.83	2.04 / 2.78	2.00 / 2.71	1.98 / 2.68	1.95 / 2.62	1.93 / 2.59	1.92 / 2.57

degrees of freedom (denominator)

Critical Values of F (Probabilities of 5 and 1 Percent)

Each cell shows the 5% critical value (top) over the 1% critical value (bottom).

df																								
19	4.38/8.18	3.52/5.93	3.13/5.01	2.90/4.50	2.74/4.17	2.63/3.94	2.55/3.77	2.48/3.63	2.43/3.52	2.38/3.43	2.34/3.36	2.31/3.30	2.26/3.19	2.21/3.12	2.15/3.00	2.11/2.92	2.07/2.84	2.02/2.76	2.00/2.70	1.96/2.63	1.94/2.60	1.91/2.54	1.90/2.51	1.88/2.49
20	4.35/8.10	3.49/5.85	3.10/4.94	2.87/4.43	2.71/4.10	2.60/3.87	2.52/3.71	2.45/3.56	2.40/3.45	2.35/3.37	2.31/3.30	2.28/3.23	2.23/3.13	2.18/3.05	2.12/2.94	2.08/2.86	2.04/2.77	1.99/2.69	1.96/2.63	1.92/2.56	1.90/2.53	1.87/2.47	1.85/2.44	1.84/2.42
21	4.32/8.02	3.47/5.78	3.07/4.87	2.84/4.37	2.68/4.04	2.57/3.81	2.49/3.65	2.42/3.51	2.37/3.40	2.32/3.31	2.28/3.24	2.25/3.17	2.20/3.07	2.15/2.99	2.09/2.88	2.05/2.80	2.00/2.72	1.96/2.63	1.93/2.58	1.89/2.51	1.87/2.47	1.84/2.42	1.82/2.38	1.81/2.36
22	4.30/7.94	3.44/5.72	3.05/4.82	2.82/4.31	2.66/3.99	2.55/3.76	2.47/3.59	2.40/3.45	2.35/3.35	2.30/3.26	2.26/3.18	2.23/3.12	2.18/3.02	2.13/2.94	2.07/2.83	2.03/2.75	1.98/2.67	1.93/2.58	1.91/2.53	1.87/2.46	1.84/2.42	1.81/2.37	1.80/2.33	1.78/2.31
23	4.28/7.88	3.42/5.66	3.03/4.76	2.80/4.26	2.64/3.94	2.53/3.71	2.45/3.54	2.38/3.41	2.32/3.30	2.28/3.21	2.24/3.14	2.20/3.07	2.14/2.97	2.10/2.89	2.04/2.78	2.00/2.70	1.96/2.62	1.91/2.53	1.88/2.48	1.84/2.41	1.82/2.37	1.79/2.32	1.77/2.28	1.76/2.26
24	4.26/7.82	3.40/5.61	3.01/4.72	2.78/4.22	2.62/3.90	2.51/3.67	2.43/3.50	2.36/3.36	2.30/3.25	2.26/3.17	2.22/3.09	2.18/3.03	2.13/2.93	2.09/2.85	2.02/2.74	1.98/2.66	1.94/2.58	1.89/2.49	1.86/2.44	1.82/2.36	1.80/2.33	1.76/2.27	1.74/2.23	1.73/2.21
25	4.24/7.77	3.38/5.57	2.99/4.68	2.76/4.18	2.60/3.86	2.49/3.63	2.41/3.46	2.34/3.32	2.28/3.21	2.24/3.13	2.20/3.05	2.16/2.99	2.11/2.89	2.06/2.81	2.00/2.70	1.96/2.62	1.92/2.54	1.87/2.45	1.84/2.40	1.80/2.32	1.77/2.29	1.74/2.23	1.72/2.19	1.71/2.17
26	4.22/7.72	3.37/5.53	2.98/4.64	2.74/4.14	2.59/3.82	2.47/3.59	2.39/3.42	2.32/3.29	2.27/3.17	2.22/3.09	2.18/3.02	2.15/2.96	2.10/2.86	2.05/2.77	1.99/2.66	1.95/2.58	1.90/2.50	1.85/2.41	1.82/2.36	1.78/2.28	1.76/2.25	1.72/2.19	1.70/2.15	1.69/2.13
27	4.21/7.68	3.35/5.49	2.96/4.60	2.73/4.11	2.57/3.79	2.46/3.56	2.37/3.39	2.30/3.26	2.25/3.14	2.20/3.06	2.16/2.98	2.13/2.93	2.08/2.83	2.03/2.74	1.97/2.63	1.93/2.55	1.88/2.47	1.84/2.38	1.80/2.33	1.76/2.25	1.74/2.21	1.71/2.16	1.68/2.12	1.67/2.10
28	4.20/7.64	3.34/5.45	2.95/4.57	2.71/4.07	2.56/3.76	2.44/3.53	2.36/3.36	2.29/3.23	2.24/3.11	2.19/3.03	2.15/2.95	2.12/2.90	2.06/2.80	2.02/2.71	1.96/2.60	1.91/2.52	1.87/2.44	1.81/2.35	1.78/2.30	1.75/2.22	1.72/2.18	1.69/2.13	1.67/2.09	1.65/2.06
29	4.18/7.60	3.33/5.42	2.93/4.54	2.70/4.04	2.54/3.73	2.43/3.50	2.35/3.33	2.28/3.20	2.22/3.08	2.18/3.00	2.14/2.92	2.10/2.87	2.05/2.77	2.00/2.68	1.94/2.57	1.90/2.49	1.85/2.41	1.80/2.32	1.77/2.27	1.73/2.19	1.71/2.15	1.68/2.10	1.65/2.06	1.64/2.03
30	4.17/7.56	3.32/5.39	2.92/4.51	2.69/4.02	2.53/3.70	2.42/3.47	2.34/3.30	2.27/3.17	2.21/3.06	2.16/2.98	2.12/2.90	2.09/2.84	2.04/2.74	1.99/2.66	1.93/2.55	1.89/2.47	1.84/2.38	1.79/2.29	1.76/2.24	1.72/2.16	1.69/2.13	1.66/2.07	1.64/2.03	1.62/2.01
32	4.15/7.50	3.30/5.34	2.90/4.46	2.67/3.97	2.51/3.66	2.40/3.42	2.32/3.25	2.25/3.12	2.19/3.01	2.14/2.94	2.10/2.86	2.07/2.80	2.02/2.70	1.97/2.62	1.91/2.51	1.86/2.42	1.82/2.34	1.76/2.25	1.74/2.20	1.69/2.12	1.67/2.08	1.64/2.02	1.61/1.98	1.59/1.96
34	4.13/7.44	3.28/5.29	2.88/4.42	2.65/3.93	2.49/3.61	2.38/3.38	2.30/3.21	2.23/3.08	2.17/2.97	2.12/2.89	2.08/2.82	2.05/2.76	2.00/2.66	1.95/2.58	1.89/2.47	1.84/2.38	1.80/2.30	1.74/2.21	1.71/2.15	1.67/2.08	1.64/2.04	1.61/1.98	1.59/1.94	1.57/1.91
36	4.11/7.39	3.26/5.25	2.86/4.38	2.63/3.89	2.48/3.58	2.36/3.35	2.28/3.18	2.21/3.04	2.15/2.94	2.10/2.86	2.06/2.78	2.03/2.72	1.98/2.62	1.93/2.54	1.87/2.43	1.82/2.35	1.78/2.26	1.72/2.17	1.69/2.12	1.65/2.04	1.62/2.00	1.59/1.94	1.56/1.90	1.55/1.87
38	4.10/7.35	3.25/5.21	2.85/4.34	2.62/3.86	2.46/3.54	2.35/3.32	2.26/3.15	2.19/3.02	2.14/2.91	2.09/2.82	2.05/2.75	2.02/2.69	1.96/2.59	1.92/2.51	1.85/2.40	1.80/2.32	1.76/2.22	1.71/2.14	1.67/2.08	1.63/2.00	1.60/1.97	1.57/1.90	1.54/1.86	1.53/1.84
40	4.07/7.31	3.23/5.18	2.84/4.31	2.61/3.83	2.45/3.51	2.34/3.29	2.25/3.12	2.18/2.99	2.12/2.88	2.07/2.80	2.04/2.73	2.00/2.66	1.95/2.56	1.90/2.49	1.84/2.37	1.79/2.29	1.74/2.20	1.69/2.11	1.66/2.05	1.61/1.97	1.59/1.94	1.55/1.88	1.53/1.84	1.51/1.81

degrees of freedom (denominator)

(continued)

Critical Values of F (Probabilities of 5 and 1 Percent)

df (denom) \ df (numerator)	1	2	3	4	5	6	7	8	9	10	11	12	14	16	20	24	30	40	50	75	100	200	500	∞
42	4.07 / 7.27	3.22 / 5.15	2.83 / 4.29	2.59 / 3.80	2.44 / 3.49	2.32 / 3.26	2.24 / 3.10	2.17 / 2.96	2.11 / 2.86	2.06 / 2.77	2.02 / 2.70	1.99 / 2.64	1.94 / 2.54	1.89 / 2.46	1.82 / 2.35	1.78 / 2.26	1.73 / 2.17	1.68 / 2.08	1.64 / 2.02	1.60 / 1.94	1.57 / 1.91	1.54 / 1.85	1.51 / 1.80	1.49 / 1.78
44	4.06 / 7.24	3.21 / 5.12	2.82 / 4.26	2.58 / 3.78	2.43 / 3.46	2.31 / 3.24	2.23 / 3.07	2.16 / 2.94	2.10 / 2.84	2.05 / 2.75	2.01 / 2.68	1.98 / 2.62	1.92 / 2.52	1.88 / 2.44	1.81 / 2.32	1.76 / 2.24	1.72 / 2.15	1.66 / 2.06	1.63 / 2.00	1.58 / 1.92	1.56 / 1.88	1.52 / 1.82	1.50 / 1.78	1.48 / 1.75
46	4.05 / 7.21	3.20 / 5.10	2.81 / 4.24	2.57 / 3.76	2.42 / 3.44	2.30 / 3.22	2.22 / 3.05	2.14 / 2.92	2.09 / 2.82	2.04 / 2.73	2.00 / 2.66	1.97 / 2.60	1.91 / 2.50	1.87 / 2.42	1.80 / 2.30	1.75 / 2.22	1.71 / 2.13	1.65 / 2.04	1.62 / 1.98	1.57 / 1.90	1.54 / 1.86	1.51 / 1.80	1.48 / 1.76	1.46 / 1.72
48	4.04 / 7.19	3.19 / 5.08	2.80 / 4.22	2.56 / 3.74	2.41 / 3.42	2.30 / 3.20	2.21 / 3.04	2.14 / 2.90	2.08 / 2.80	2.03 / 2.71	1.99 / 2.64	1.96 / 2.58	1.90 / 2.48	1.86 / 2.40	1.79 / 2.28	1.74 / 2.20	1.70 / 2.11	1.64 / 2.02	1.61 / 1.96	1.56 / 1.88	1.53 / 1.84	1.50 / 1.78	1.47 / 1.73	1.45 / 1.70
50	4.03 / 7.17	3.18 / 5.06	2.79 / 4.20	2.56 / 3.72	2.40 / 3.41	2.29 / 3.18	2.20 / 3.02	2.13 / 2.88	2.07 / 2.78	2.02 / 2.70	1.98 / 2.62	1.95 / 2.56	1.90 / 2.46	1.85 / 2.39	1.78 / 2.26	1.74 / 2.18	1.69 / 2.10	1.63 / 2.00	1.60 / 1.94	1.55 / 1.86	1.52 / 1.82	1.48 / 1.76	1.46 / 1.71	1.44 / 1.68
55	4.02 / 7.12	3.17 / 5.01	2.78 / 4.16	2.54 / 3.68	2.38 / 3.37	2.27 / 3.15	2.18 / 2.98	2.11 / 2.85	2.05 / 2.75	2.00 / 2.66	1.97 / 2.59	1.93 / 2.53	1.88 / 2.43	1.83 / 2.35	1.76 / 2.23	1.72 / 2.15	1.67 / 2.06	1.61 / 1.96	1.58 / 1.90	1.52 / 1.82	1.50 / 1.78	1.46 / 1.71	1.43 / 1.66	1.41 / 1.64
60	4.00 / 7.08	3.15 / 4.98	2.76 / 4.13	2.52 / 3.65	2.37 / 3.34	2.25 / 3.12	2.17 / 2.95	2.10 / 2.82	2.04 / 2.72	1.99 / 2.63	1.95 / 2.56	1.92 / 2.50	1.86 / 2.40	1.81 / 2.32	1.75 / 2.20	1.70 / 2.12	1.65 / 2.03	1.59 / 1.93	1.56 / 1.87	1.50 / 1.79	1.48 / 1.74	1.44 / 1.68	1.41 / 1.63	1.39 / 1.60
65	3.99 / 7.04	3.14 / 4.95	2.75 / 4.10	2.51 / 3.62	2.36 / 3.31	2.24 / 3.09	2.15 / 2.93	2.08 / 2.79	2.02 / 2.70	1.98 / 2.61	1.94 / 2.54	1.90 / 2.47	1.85 / 2.37	1.80 / 2.30	1.73 / 2.18	1.68 / 2.09	1.63 / 2.00	1.57 / 1.90	1.54 / 1.84	1.49 / 1.76	1.46 / 1.71	1.42 / 1.64	1.39 / 1.60	1.37 / 1.56
70	3.98 / 7.01	3.13 / 4.92	2.74 / 4.08	2.50 / 3.60	2.35 / 3.29	2.23 / 3.07	2.14 / 2.91	2.07 / 2.77	2.01 / 2.67	1.97 / 2.59	1.93 / 2.51	1.89 / 2.45	1.84 / 2.35	1.79 / 2.28	1.72 / 2.15	1.67 / 2.07	1.62 / 1.98	1.56 / 1.88	1.53 / 1.82	1.47 / 1.74	1.45 / 1.69	1.40 / 1.62	1.37 / 1.56	1.35 / 1.53
80	3.96 / 6.96	3.11 / 4.88	2.72 / 4.04	2.48 / 3.56	2.33 / 3.25	2.21 / 3.04	2.12 / 2.87	2.05 / 2.74	1.99 / 2.64	1.95 / 2.55	1.91 / 2.48	1.88 / 2.41	1.82 / 2.32	1.77 / 2.24	1.70 / 2.11	1.65 / 2.03	1.60 / 1.94	1.54 / 1.84	1.51 / 1.78	1.45 / 1.70	1.42 / 1.65	1.38 / 1.57	1.35 / 1.52	1.32 / 1.49
100	3.94 / 6.90	3.09 / 4.82	2.70 / 3.98	2.46 / 3.51	2.30 / 3.20	2.19 / 2.99	2.10 / 2.82	2.03 / 2.69	1.97 / 2.59	1.92 / 2.51	1.88 / 2.43	1.85 / 2.36	1.79 / 2.26	1.75 / 2.19	1.68 / 2.06	1.63 / 1.98	1.57 / 1.89	1.51 / 1.79	1.48 / 1.73	1.42 / 1.64	1.39 / 1.59	1.34 / 1.51	1.30 / 1.46	1.28 / 1.43
125	3.92 / 6.84	3.07 / 4.78	2.68 / 3.94	2.44 / 3.47	2.29 / 3.17	2.17 / 2.95	2.08 / 2.79	2.01 / 2.65	1.95 / 2.56	1.90 / 2.47	1.86 / 2.40	1.83 / 2.33	1.77 / 2.23	1.72 / 2.15	1.65 / 2.03	1.60 / 1.94	1.55 / 1.85	1.49 / 1.75	1.45 / 1.68	1.39 / 1.59	1.36 / 1.54	1.31 / 1.46	1.27 / 1.40	1.25 / 1.37
150	3.91 / 6.81	3.06 / 4.75	2.67 / 3.91	2.43 / 3.44	2.27 / 3.14	2.16 / 2.92	2.07 / 2.76	2.00 / 2.62	1.94 / 2.53	1.89 / 2.44	1.85 / 2.37	1.82 / 2.30	1.76 / 2.20	1.71 / 2.12	1.64 / 2.00	1.59 / 1.91	1.54 / 1.83	1.47 / 1.72	1.44 / 1.66	1.37 / 1.56	1.34 / 1.51	1.29 / 1.43	1.25 / 1.37	1.22 / 1.33
200	3.89 / 6.76	3.04 / 4.71	2.65 / 3.88	2.41 / 3.41	2.26 / 3.11	2.14 / 2.90	2.05 / 2.73	1.98 / 2.60	1.92 / 2.50	1.87 / 2.41	1.83 / 2.34	1.80 / 2.28	1.74 / 2.17	1.69 / 2.09	1.62 / 1.97	1.57 / 1.88	1.52 / 1.79	1.45 / 1.69	1.42 / 1.62	1.35 / 1.53	1.32 / 1.48	1.26 / 1.39	1.22 / 1.33	1.19 / 1.28
400	3.86 / 6.70	3.02 / 4.66	2.62 / 3.83	2.39 / 3.36	2.23 / 3.06	2.12 / 2.85	2.03 / 2.69	1.96 / 2.55	1.90 / 2.46	1.85 / 2.37	1.81 / 2.29	1.78 / 2.23	1.72 / 2.12	1.67 / 2.04	1.60 / 1.92	1.54 / 1.84	1.49 / 1.74	1.42 / 1.64	1.38 / 1.57	1.32 / 1.47	1.28 / 1.42	1.22 / 1.32	1.16 / 1.24	1.13 / 1.19
1000	3.85 / 6.66	3.00 / 4.62	2.61 / 3.80	2.38 / 3.34	2.22 / 3.04	2.10 / 2.82	2.02 / 2.66	1.95 / 2.53	1.89 / 2.43	1.84 / 2.34	1.80 / 2.26	1.76 / 2.20	1.70 / 2.09	1.65 / 2.01	1.58 / 1.89	1.53 / 1.81	1.47 / 1.71	1.41 / 1.61	1.36 / 1.54	1.30 / 1.44	1.26 / 1.38	1.19 / 1.28	1.13 / 1.19	1.08 / 1.11
∞	3.84 / 6.64	2.99 / 4.60	2.60 / 3.78	2.37 / 3.32	2.21 / 3.02	2.09 / 2.80	2.01 / 2.64	1.94 / 2.51	1.88 / 2.41	1.83 / 2.32	1.79 / 2.24	1.75 / 2.18	1.69 / 2.07	1.64 / 1.99	1.57 / 1.87	1.52 / 1.79	1.46 / 1.69	1.40 / 1.59	1.35 / 1.52	1.28 / 1.41	1.24 / 1.36	1.17 / 1.25	1.11 / 1.15	1.00 / 1.00

degrees of freedom (denominator)